T0196403

RESPONDING TO THE CALL

ANDREW L. SMITH

WESTBOW
PRESS®
A DIVISION OF THOMAS NELSON
& ZONDERVAN

WestBow Press books may be ordered through booksellers or by contacting:

WestBow Press
A Division of Thomas Nelson & Zondervan
1663 Liberty Drive
Bloomington, IN 47403
www.westbowpress.com
844-714-3454

Scripture taken from the King James Version of the Bible.

ISBN: 978-1-6642-1790-4 (sc)
ISBN: 978-1-6642-1792-8 (hc)
ISBN: 978-1-6642-1791-1 (e)

Library of Congress Control Number: 2020926003

Print information available on the last page.

WestBow Press rev. date: 02/09/2021

CONTENTS

INTRODUCTION vii
PREFACE.. ix

SECTION ONE..1

  1. CONVERSION 3
  2. MT. VERNON BAPTIST CHURCH..................... 5
  3. THE ROSEBUD 7
  4. THE CALL.. 9
  5. STRIPES...11
  6. FIRST CHURCHES 13
  7. STONE LICK..15
  8. READY...17
  9. DRAFTED...19
 10. CLEAR CREEK 20
 11. KAYJAY 23
 12. FOUR MILE MINE................................... 25
 13. CUBAGE 28
 14. THE FLAT LICK REVIVAL 31
 15. CAMP PATTERSON 33
 16. CALIFORNIA.. 35
 17. THE CELEBRATION 39
 18. RETIREMENT....................................... 41

SECTION TWO...47

  1. GOING TO COLLEGE 49
  2. GEORGIA TECH 52
  3. CLAIRMONT BAPTIST CHURCH 58
  4. BUFORD HIGHWAY BAPTIST CHURCH 61
  5. YORUBA 63
  6. DUNWOODY 65
  7. HOSPITALITY 71
  8. ORDINATION.......................................74
  9. SLEEPING DEACONS 75
 10. THE CAT.. 77

11. THE FUNERAL 80
12. DUNWOODY 84

SECTION THREE 93

1. BROOKS RAMSEY 95
2. JAMES HATLEY 98
3. THE PRODIGAL SON 99
4. HATLEY'S OFFICE 101
5. IT WORKS 104
6. THE TRUTH 107
7. CHORES 111
8. LIFE AND DEATH 114
9. MUSIC IN THE RAFTERS 117
10. THE GRACE OF TALENTS 119
11. BE CAREFUL DAD 121
12. BRAZIL 124
13. THE GUN 127
14. COWBOYS AND INDIANS 130
15. INTO THE DEEP 134
16. FOUR REASONS 135
17. GREAT GREAT GRANDPAPPY 137
18. STUPID 139
19. YOU SURE DO LOOK GOOD 141
20. NOT YOUR PROBLEM 144
21. VERNON GREEN 153

POSTSCRIPT 157

INTRODUCTION

My previous books are writings that some people call poems, some say they are free verse but to me they are simply writings.

This book contains some of the stories I have recorded or written over the past 60 years. The "string" that laces them together is what many people in the church say is a "call." A call presents itself in many different ways.

Sometimes it is a feeling that God wants you to do something, to be something, to change, to go somewhere. The feeling can start small and then intensify over time until it must be answered. That is the way my father experienced the call to be a preacher. (It is interesting that prior to the late twentieth century it was a call "to preach.") The ministry, the pastorate was secondary to the call "to preach."

We now understand that the call can be for many ways to minister in the Kingdom of God. In my father's life it was not only the call to preach, it was the call to go to school, the call to be the pastor of several churches, the call to start churches in California and many other calls that changed his life.

These stories include the call to Dr. A. Scott Patterson to go back to a yellow fever infested Nigeria to be sure that many years of missionary effort would not be lost. The call to Dr. Albert Schweitzer to go to Africa to "Repay the grace of talents." In his case the call was as much intellectual as it was spiritual.

My call to be the pastor of a small semi-rural church was both specific and limited. My call to be an architect was just as important as the call to be a pastor. And, it can be argued that the call to go to Louisiana to listen to a man who was trying to find his way back to the Lord was just as much a call as any other.

Sometimes the question is not. "Is the Lord calling?"
The questions is, "Are you listening?"

Andrew Smith
April 20, 2020

PREFACE

WHEN YOUR NAME IS SMITH, YOU HAVE TO ACCEPT THE FACT THAT YOU are not able to trace your family history back very far. After three or four generations you find that your great, great, great grandfather, is one of a several Smiths from the same region of the country. There is no way you can know which Smith was your great, great, great grandfather.

We can trace our Smith linage back to the Revolutionary War but beyond that it is lost. In the early 1800s, my great, great grandfather. Jared Smith, moved to the Pigeon Forge/Wear's Valley part of East Tennessee. That area is in the foothills of the Great Smoky Mountains.

We know that another of our forbearers was Colonel Samuel T. Ware, was one of the early settlers of the area. He built Ware's Fort in what is now Pigeon Forge, Tennessee. Later he was the captain of a company of "Over the Mountain Men" who fought in the Battle of Kings Mountain.

When the U. S. Government forced the relocation of the Native Americans, a vast area of land became available for homesteading. Several families from Pigeon Forge/Wear's Valley migrated to Northwest Georgia. My great grandfather, Alferd Smith, was part of that migration. He settled in a small village called Varnell which is a few miles north of Dalton, Georgia.

My grandfather, John Jefferson Smith, Sr. was born in 1862. His wife, LouVinne Eslanger, was from another of the families that migrated to Varnell.

The Smiths, like many other families in the south, were subsistence farmers. They grew enough cash crops, (cotton and wheat) to provide money to buy shoes, plows, and other essentials, and otherwise lived off of what could be grown on the farm.

By the 1920s there were more farm boys than there were non-farm jobs. My father, along with many other young men went north to find work. He worked in the Chevrolet assembly plant in Cincinnati, Ohio for 18 years. When he was 31 years old he answered the call to preach.

The First Section of stories is about my father and his ministry.

The Second Section is stories from my ministry as the pastor of a small semi-rural church in what is now a suburb of Atlanta, Georgia.

The Third Section is stories from my experience as a member of Second Baptist Church in Memphis, Tennessee.

Andrew Smith, 2020

SECTION ONE

When I realized my parents were reaching the age when memory begins to fade, I started taking a tape recorder with me when I went to see them. I would say, "Tell me again about your call to be a preacher." I would click on the recorder and later type the story. The stories are pure oral history. They have been edited only as much as necessary for accuracy and clarity.

1. CONVERSION
2. MT. VERNON BAPTIST CHURCH
3. THE ROSEBUD
4. THE CALL
5. STRIPES
6. FIRST CHURCHES
7. STONELICK
8. READY
9. DRAFTED
10. CLEAR CREEK
11. KAYJAY
12. FOUR MILE MINE
13. CUBAGE
14. FLAT LICK
15. CAMP PATTERSON
16. CALIFORNIA
17. RETIREMENT
18. THE CELEBRATION

CONVERSION

I DON'T REMEMBER BEING CONCERNED ABOUT MY SALVATION UNTIL I was about sixteen years old. I went to church with my mother and I read the Bible but nobody ever said anything to me about being saved.

About a year before I was saved, (dad must have been worried about me) dad said, "Johnny, hitch up old Dan and take your mother to church." I let my mother out in front of the church and took old Dan and the buggy out into the oak grove and tied him up. When I got back to the door of the church, I heard my mother requesting prayer for me to be saved. That was when I came under conviction.

My brother Ben, who was seven years older than me, married a beautiful girl named Amy Hawkins. There was very little courtship; Ben was a man of few words and Amy was ready to get married. Amy was a fine Christian girl. She played the organ at the church. About six weeks after they married Amy got sick. She had meningitis, then pneumonia and finally sleeping sickness. She went into a coma for five days and died. Her sickness and death had a lasting affect on me.

Ben naturally took it very hard. He went three weeks without eating much at all. He lost over 15 pounds. One night, after supper, dad was talking to him. Dad said, "Ben, you are going to have to stop grieving. Amy is dead and there is nothing you can do that will ever bring her back." Ben said, "I'm not grieving about Amy. I know that she is in heaven. It is me that I'm worried about. I'm not saved and I can't go to heaven to be with her."

Dad said, "Ben that's between you and the good Lord." Mother was in the kitchen. When she overheard him, she came out, taking off her apron, and reaching for the family Bible. She said, "Ben, let's go into the bedroom. Get on your knees and let's get this settled." Ben got down on his knees and started praying and crying. Mother was trying to show him, in the Bible, how to be saved. I don't know if mother was just nervous and excited or whether she couldn't find the scripture she was looking for. Finally she said, "Johnny come here and find that Scripture that says, 'Come unto me all ye who are weary and heavy laden and I will give you rest.'"

I found the passage and gave it to her. She read it to Ben and Ben was saved. My mother nearly shouted the house down.

Ben and me made a crop that summer. Ben's conversion and Amy's death and knowing that my mother was praying for me to be saved, laid heavy on my mind. Ben would witness to me as we walked to Mt. Vernon Baptist Church.

That fall, when the crops were laid by, they had the annual revival. I was under conviction but I didn't quite know what to do. One night after the service was over, Mrs. Sally Partison came to me and said, "Johnny, don't you want to give your heart to Jesus?" I said, "I sure do." The next night I went forward and was saved. I remember that the preacher was named Darnell. I joined Smith's Chapel Methodist Church.

_____

JOHN J. SMITH

MT. VERNON BAPTIST CHURCH

In the spring of 1927 I went to Ohio to go to work in the Chevrolet assembly plant. In the fall of 1928 there was a long layoff. That was the beginning of the depression. I came home and stayed about three months. The revival at Mt Vernon that fall was preached by William [W. L.] Tallent. Preacher Tallent lived in Chattanooga and had to be driven 25 miles to the church. He was not always on time. He said, "Johnny, if I'm late you start the singing and take care of the service until I get there." That was my first experience taking a leadership role in church. The 1928 revival was the most significant event at Mt. Vernon Church for many years. There were 51 decisions for Christ, 38 of them were for baptism. More people joined the church than there were people attending the church.

After the revival the men of the church came to me and said, "Johnny, you be our Sunday School teacher." I had never taught a class and had no idea what to do or how to do it. The class was a group of old men with white chin whiskers and I was only 21 years old. There was no literature so I simply started with the first verse of the first chapter of Matthew.

My brother Emmitt was saved when he was 19 and I was 21. Mother was very burdened for him because he was the only one of her children who had not been saved. One night during the revival, Emmitt went to the altar. Mother and I were right behind him. We prayed with him and he was saved. My mother was kneeling beside every one of her children when they were saved.

I was driving a 1925 Chevrolet cabriolet with a rumble seat. Mother heard us talking about the rumble seat and she decided that she would ride home in the rumble seat. Ben was in the seat with her. About half way home mother got happy all over again and started shouting and praising the Lord. When she started shouting, she couldn't sit still. I hollered for Ben to keep her from jumping out of the car. I pulled over to the side of the road. We got out of the car, got on our knees and prayed until mother calmed down.

A week or two later my brothers, Jack and Emmitt and I were baptized in the creek down close to Keith school. There were 17 baptized that day. The preacher and his nephew, who led the singing, did the baptizing. They were both short and Emmitt was a little over six feet and four inches tall. They kept backing out into the creek trying to find water deep enough to baptize Emmitt. They tried once and couldn't get all of him under the water. One of them stepped into a deep hole and we thought he was going to drown.

After we joined the Baptist church, mother went to church with us. She attended the Baptist church for 20 years but she remained a Methodist.

JOHN J. SMITH

THE ROSEBUD

DURING THE DEPRESSION THE CHEVROLET PLANT WOULD CLOSE down for several weeks at a time. When I was laid off I would go back to Georgia and stay with my parents.

Mount Vernon Baptist Church had a special service once each year they called "Appreciation Day." They held the service when the roses were blooming. They put a large pile of roses on the table at the front of the church. At the end of the service people would go get a rose and pin it on someone who had been a blessing to them. I got a rosebud and pinned it on Aunt Sally Partison and thanked her for telling me about Jesus.

People started pinning roses on my mother. They pinned so many roses on her that they ran out of pins. People still came and dropped the roses in her lap. It wasn't long before her cup was full and running over (she was an old fashioned shouting Methodist) and she started shouting and running up and down the aisle. Roses went everywhere.

Your mother and I married in May of 1932 and moved to Cincinnati, Ohio. Seven years later I answered the call to preach. I only had an eight grade education and knew that if I was going to be a preacher I needed more education. I studied at Clear Creek Mountain Preacher's School for three years.

When I finished school, we moved to Tennessee and then to Georgia and then back to Tennessee. I was the pastor of several churches and I established a children's Bible camp but in 1958 the Lord called me to a new work. I answered a call to be a pioneer missionary in California. On January the 4th, 1958, I loaded your mother and all we could cram into a 1957 Plymouth and went to California. I became the pastor of a new church that was meeting in an abandoned night club.

Every year, we drove back to Georgia see our families. We went to see your grandmother Lowery who was living in a nursing home in Dalton, Georgia. We visited with her and were about to leave when someone said, "John, do you know that Aunt Sally Partison is still alive and is living in this nursing home?"

I found her. She was 96 years old. I went down to her room to talk to her. I was glad to see her. I thanked her again for telling me about Jesus. When our visit was over and I was turning to go away, she said, "Johnny, hand me my Bible." There between the pages of her Bible was the little rosebud that I had given her thirty years ago. She had kept it pressed in her Bible all that time.

Aunt Sally was not an outstanding church worker and she lived the hard life of a common country woman. But, she had a testimony for the Lord and she loved people. When she saw a young man who needed a little encouragement to help him decide to give his heart to the Lord she simply said, "Johnny, don't you want to give your heart to Jesus?"

That rosebud pressed between the pages of an old woman's bible is an example of the two most important elements in the Christian life.

First is that anybody can care about people and anybody can, in their own way, tell people about Jesus. That is what Aunt Sally did. She did what she could for Jesus. She was just a sun bonneted country woman who grubbed a meager living out of a small farm but she was always ready to give her testimony for the Lord.

The second lesson is that the support and encouragement that comes from saying thank you is what Christian fellowship is all about. You never know when a quite word of encouragement is going to change someone's entire life. You never know when a sincere "thank you" is going to be treasured for a life time.

They called it "Appreciation Day" and they filled my mother's lap with roses. She got happy and scattered roses all over the church. She probably didn't think much about it after it was all over. To her it was "Appreciation Day".

I pinned one little rosebud on Aunt Sally and thanked her for encouraging me to give my heart to Jesus and she remembered it for the rest of her life. To her it was "Appreciation Thirty Years."

John J. Smith

THE CALL

When we first moved to Ohio, we didn't go to church on a regular basis. We would go on special occasions and when we went home we would go to Mt. Vernon Baptist. When we moved from Norwood to Amelia, Ohio, to a house we called the Old Temple place, there was a small church right across the road. We moved because I came home from work one day and found you pulling your little red wagon right down the middle of the street. I started looking for a place out in the country. I wanted a safer place to raise children.

About a year later, I began to take you and your brother to Sunday School at the little church across the road. It wasn't long before they asked me to teach a class of boys. We didn't have preaching every Sunday. We would have a preacher two times a month. After I had been teaching for a while, old brother Coombs, who was the senior deacon, asked me to lead the singing and have a devotion when we did not have a preacher. I remember that one Sunday afternoon three or four churches gathered for a singing and preaching service and I moderated the event. That was when I began to feel the call to preach.

When your brother, Don, was 4 years old he came down with pneumonia. An old Methodist preacher came to see him. I met him out in front of the house. He said, "How's my boy? How's my boy today?" I said, "He's better, he's going to be OK. I'm the one that needs you." We were walking back to the house and he said, "What's wrong with you?" I said, "I've got to preach." By the time I got to the word preach I had started bawling and the word preach came out, "preeeeeech".

Your mother and I had stayed up to midnight the night before as I tried to convince her that God was calling me to preach. I asked her if she thought God could make a preacher out of me. She said that she didn't see how in the world he could do it.

Gertie came out of the house, wiping her hands on her apron, and the old preacher said, "Now let's get in here and settle this." He wasn't much of a preacher but he was a wise old man. We went into Don's bedroom and got on our knees and prayed until we got some peace.

Later, he talked to me about the stress of being a preacher. He told me about all the hardships and disappointments in the ministry. He said that the ministry can break your heart. He talked to me for over an hour, just as hard as he could talk, then he said, "Do you still want to preach?" I told him that I didn't have to preach but that I would rather die than to go on living with the call to preach and not do it. He said that was what he wanted to hear.

Sometime later my brother Jack asked his pastor to ask me to preach a revival. I made plans to go back to Tennessee and preach the revival. I told my pastor about it. One Sunday afternoon after the service he came out to the car and said he wanted to give a book. It was a book of sermons. I didn't know there was such a thing as a book of sermons. I told him I didn't think I needed it. I said. "The Lord has laid a sermon on my heart that is burning a hole in it! I feel like my heart is going to burst if I don't get to preach it!" He said, "Well, any old spring might go dry. Take this book, you never know when you might need it."

I found out, after I told every one that I had accepted the call to preach, that my mother had been praying for years that the Lord would call me to preach. She said that she had vowed not to tell me because she didn't want her prayers to call me to preach. She wanted the Lord to do it.

JOHN J. SMITH

STRIPES

ON A COLD NIGHT, IN THE WINTER OF 1906, LOUVINNIE SMITH snuggled up to her husband and said, "John, we are going to have another baby." John said that if he was going to be a father again, he wanted the baby to be a boy and he wanted him to have his name. Lou Vinnie said silently, to herself, that if she was going to be a mother again, she wanted the baby to be a boy and she wanted him to be a preacher.

Little Johnnie knew all his life that he had a special relationship with his mother but he did not know why. He struggled with the Lord's call until he was 31 years old, He answered the call to preach in 1938. His mother's secret prayers for 32 years were answered. Only then did she tell him.

His first revival was at Old Sugar Creek Baptist Church in southeast Tennessee. It was the same church his grandfather and grandmother belonged to after the Civil War.

The revival went very well but the church had one burden that had not been lifted. They had been praying a long time for an old farmer in the community who would get drunk and beat his wife and children. He came several nights and sat in the back of the church. He was under such deep conviction that he would grip the back of the pew as if he were trying to squeeze it into sawdust. Great tears would roll down his cheeks but he would just bow his head and hold on to the pew. On the last night of the revival he gave in and came forward to the mourner's bench and started to pray. By the time he got to the altar the whole front of the church was full of people praying with him. They all prayed at the same time and they all prayed out loud.

The young preacher made his way from behind the pulpit to kneel beside the old man. He opened his Bible to the 53rd chapter of Isaiah. Very quietly he began to read to him;

> *"He was wounded for our transgressions, He was bruised for our iniquities ... and with His stripes we are healed."*

That old gray haired man took his knarled and broken fingers and put them on the Bible and began to move his fingers along the Scripture. He said, "Read it to me again, Johnny. Read it to me again." Johnny read it again;

> *"He was wounded for our transgressions, He was bruised*
> *for our inequities ... and with His stripes we are healed."*

The old man said, "Preacher, I believe it! I believe it!"

—————————————

ANDREW SMITH

FIRST CHURCHES

UNCLE ALBERT COOMBS CAME OVER TO WHERE WE WERE BUILDING the house on ten mile road. He said that a church was trying to get in touch with me. Uncle Albert was a fellow deacon in the Lindale Baptist Church. In fact we were the only deacons. He was the senior deacon and I was the junior deacon. He said that I should call Brother Cecil Ingram. Brother Ingram had been the pastor of Carthage Baptist Church but had accepted a call to another church.

He asked me if I would preach at Carthage. I was happy to have an opportunity to preach. The church was in an old fashion building that was not constructed as a Baptist building. The choir sat up in a loft. They looked like a bunch of chickens going up to roost. The pulpit was over on the side. I thought I was preaching in an Episcopal church. After the service a little old lady came to me and said, "I think I know where they would like to have you as their pastor. The church is called Sugar Run."

Sugar Run was in a rural community north of Cincinnati, Ohio and about thirty miles from our home. I was the pastor of Sugar Run for about a year. I remember they had a homecoming celebration. They set up a long table in a sugar maple grove overlooking a beautiful valley. The ladies were kind of stuck up; they all lived in big fancy farm houses and were pretty well off. They brought a lot of good food and spread it out on the table but they ate their own food. They did not have the same kind of fellowship we were used to back home in Georgia.

I preached at Sugar Run two Sundays each month and the other two Sundays I preached at little church called Silver Grove. We used to go home with a couple named Adams who had children the same age as our children. She was a wonderful cook and we had a nice time but she talked constantly about her father in law. He was superintendent of the Sunday School but she talked about him as if he were a dog.

The Lord blessed our ministry at those little churches. At least they tolerated a preacher who had very little experience.

JOHN J. SMITH

I REMEMBER TWO INCIDENTS, ONE FROM EACH CHURCH. AT THE SUGAR Run church, my brother and sister got into the offering plates and played with the money.

At Silver Grove they used a common silver cup for the wine when they celebrated communion. Mother would almost choke when she had to sip from the cup after fifteen or twenty people had already sipped from it. She would not let anybody know that it bothered her but she would fuss about it all the way home.

ANDREW SMITH

STONE LICK

IN OCTOBER OF 1941 I RECEIVED A CALL TO BE THE PASTOR OF THE Stone Lick Baptist Church which is a little north of Cincinnati, Ohio. . Almost all of the young men in the church went into one branch of the service or the other. It was natural for their mothers to ask the pastor to pray for their sons. In order to keep track of everyone we put a sign in front of the church with all the names on it. Before long they had a long list of names. When other people from the area heard about the sign they wanted the names of their sons on it too. Soon the sign was 5 feet wide and 6 feet high.

The first person I ever baptized was a young man who was going off to war. He knew he might not return and he wanted to be baptized. He was going to leave the next day. We went down to the creek behind the church after the morning service. We were not prepared but we simply waded out into the creek until we found a spot deep enough and I baptized him. He was wearing his uniform and I had on my best suit, but it didn't matter, I baptized him anyway.

Later that winter, 6 or 7 people had been saved and they wanted to be baptized. It was very cold but I told them I would do it if they wanted me to. We had to break the ice in the creek. I went out into the water and the candidates came in one by one. After I baptized them, the ladies of the church threw a blanket over them and they ran up the hill to the church to change clothes. I didn't realize how cold I was until I got out of the water. I thought I was going to freeze to death.

JOHN J. SMITH

WE WERE DRIVING HOME AFTER SUNDAY MORNING SERVICE WHEN THE program on the radio was interrupted. "The Japanese have bombed Pearl Harbor." My mother said, "John, does this mean we are at war?" Dad said, "Yes Girtie, I am sure we will go to war." She got very serious and asked, "Will you have to go?" He said, "I don't know, but if they call me, I will go."

ANDREW SMITH

READY

My mother and father were born and raised in Georgia in the early part of the twentieth century. After they married they moved to Ohio and established their home in Norwood, Ohio. During the next few years they were blessed with three children. I am the oldest, my brother Don is two years younger and my little sister Jean is four years younger. In 1940 they built a new house close to Amelia, Ohio which is about 20 miles east of Cincinnati.

One clear winter evening after supper, my father was reading or perhaps dozing in his armchair and we children were listening to the Lone Ranger on the big Zenith console radio. Mother was finishing her chores in the kitchen. She looked out the window over her kitchen sink and saw something in the northern sky she had never seen before. Great streaks of light were streaming up into the sky and it was bright enough to read a newspaper outside. We all ran out into the yard to see what was happening. My mother stood close to my father. He put his arm around her and we children huddled around them.

They were from the south and had only an eighth grade education. They had never heard of the "Northern Lights." They probably didn't know until years later that the phenomenon they were seeing was the Aurora Borealis. All they knew was that the sky was full of funnel shaped lights streaming from earth to a point in the sky. My mother looked up into my father's face and said, "John, is this the Second Coming?" My father said, "I don't know Girtie but if it is we are ready."

We stood there like a little family group in a Norman Rockwell painting, waiting patiently for whatever was going to happen. Eventually the lights began to fade away and we went into the house. My father found a news report on the radio that told us the atmospheric conditions were unusually clear and that the "Northern Lights" could be seen all the way to southern Ohio.

Every time I hear people speculate about the Second Coming of Christ and make absurd claims about signs and prophecies I remember that night in Ohio and the words of Jesus:

"Therefore be ye also ready: for in such an hour as ye think not the Son of Man cometh."
Matthew 24:44

ANDREW

DRAFTED

I WAS 37 YEARS OLD IN 1944 WHEN I RECEIVED MY DRAFT NOTICE. THE
notice said that I had ten days to report to the draft board. I went the
next day and said, "Here I am, I'm ready to go."

They said, "Aren't you the pastor of Stone Lick Baptist Church?"
I said, "Yes, but I'll never hide behind the pulpit if my country needs
me." They said, "What do you want us to do?"

I said, "I'll be here in ten minuets anytime you call me to serve
my country."

They said, "We've got a partition here from your church signed by
over sixty people asking us not to draft you."

I said, "I still stand by my statement. I will be here when you need
me. I live just up the hill from here and I can be here in a flash."

They said, "We still need to decide what to do with you."

I said, "Well, if you want my opinion, I think that, if you want me
to minister to the mothers of the 48 boys we have in the war, I will stay
here and minister to them. If you want me to go to the battlefield and
minister to their sons, I'll go minister to them. You just make up your
mind. If you want me just call me."

I never heard another word from the draft board.

JOHN J. SMITH

CLEAR CREEK

In 1943 we had a revival meeting at Stone Lick Baptist Church. The preacher was from Blue Ash Baptist church. We were invited to Sunday dinner by one of the deacons. We were walking on stepping stones across a little creek in front of their house when the preacher said, "Mr. Smith, you need more training and education." I said, "I've tried, I have really tried. I talked to the president of the Moody Bible Institute. He wanted me to resign my church, come to Chicago and move my family into an apartment. I just don't think the Lord wants me to do that." "I have also talked to the president of Bob Jones College, but I didn't feel right about that either." The preacher from Blue Ash said, "I know a school, in Kentucky, that might be right for you. They will let you continue to be a pastor while you are going to school."

He gave me the name of the school and told me how to write the president, Dr. L. C. Kelly. I wrote to Dr. Kelly. He asked me to come down and visit with him. He wanted me to visit the school and talk with him before I made a decision. I visited with him but I don't remember very much about the visit. I came back home and prayed about it and wrestled with it until the first of the year. Eventually I came to the conclusion that Clear Creek was the school I should attend.

That was the biggest step I ever took. I started to school at Clear Creek Mountain Preachers School on the third day of January, 1944. They had been having a six week summer school for mountain preachers. Now they decided to have full time students. The first year there were 33 students. Five of us graduated three years later.

The first six months I was at Clear Creek, I came back home every weekend. Most of the time I rode the bus. We were in the middle of World War II and you couldn't buy enough gas to make trips like that. The bus was always crowded. Many times I had to sit on my suitcase or hang on to a strap for most of the trip. It took almost all Friday night to make the trip and then I would leave early Monday morning to go back.

The school was about five miles from Pineville, Kentucky. I don't remember how I got from Pineville out to Clear Creek. I am sure that sometimes someone from the school would pick me up. I wasn't the only preacher making weekend trips, so there were probably several of us to pick up.

When I came back to Ohio and told your mother that I thought we should sell our home and move to Clear Creek. She said, "That's all right. If that is what you believe we should do, we will do it." When I first went to Clear Creek I thought I could go to school without moving my family to Kentucky. The event that swung the pendulum was that they made me president of the class. I was older than the other students. Dr. Kelly began to depend on me to work with the young preachers. Before I knew it I was very involved with the school.

The first house we moved into at Clear Creek was down the creek from the Kelly's house. It was a summer cabin with a big screened in porch. It sat way up the hill from the road. We had to climb about 50 steps just to get to the bottom level. The main level was a story above.

Your mother's brother, Dick, came down to visit us. He said, "What did you think, John, moving your family to a place like this?" I said, "The Lord called me, Dick." He said, "He would have to call awful loud for me to hear Him, if He wanted me to move to a place like this!"

Clear Creek was a very special place. It was owned by Kentucky Baptist. It was a summer camp for children and a conference center for church leaders. In the winter it was a school for young preachers. The men, who attended Clear Creek, were men who did not have a college education. Some, like me, had never finished high school. They were men who due to finances, family, age, education or some other reason could not go through the 4 years of college and 3 years of seminary to get the traditional training for the ministry. They were called to preach and they knew that they needed more training. Clear Creek provided a place where they could get theological training and basic skills in english and pastoral counseling.

I must admit that Clear Creek was a far cry from Cincinnati, Ohio where we had lived for the past 18 years and where your mother and I raised our family. I had done well for an uneducated farm boy from Georgia. When I quit my job at the Chevrolet plant I had almost 18 years seniority.

When I told your mother that the Lord had called me to preach, she said, "John, if you are going to be a preacher I want you to be the best preacher you can possibly be." Clear Creek Bible school was the one place I had found that was open to a man, 36 years old with a 9th grade education, a wife and three children. When we sold our new house in Ohio and moved our family to Clear Creek I was sure it was the will of God. The next three years were the most unique and the most enlightening years of my life.

_____

JOHN J. SMITH

KAYJAY

SEVERAL PREACHERS FROM CLEAR CREEK MOUNTAIN PREACHERS
School tried to start a church in a mining camp called Kayjay. They
didn't have any success. A group of men were talking about it one day
and Dr. Kelly said, "You haven't talked to John Smith have you? He'll
get one started."

I said. "Where is Kayjay?" They said that you took off like you
were going to Barbourville then you went back to the west over a big
mountain.

I got a group of the preacher boys at Clear Creek to go with me
to do some door to door canvassing. The first time I took a load of
preachers to Kayjay, I pulled over to the side of the road, into one of
those places where the road widens out so two cars can pass. We could
see the whole valley spread out below us. They said, "What are you
going to do?" I said, "I am going to pray. I wouldn't attempt to go down
into that valley without knowing that the Lord was with me!"

Dr. Childs, who was the pastor of the First Baptist Church in
Barbourville said, "You are not going to go down there are you? That's
the meanest place in eastern Kentucky." He said, "Why they got to
shooting dice down there and got to gambling and got into a fight and
one of them shot another one. They just drug him out of the way. They
called for the doctor but they kept right on rolling the dice until the
law came and broke it up." I said, "They tell me that there are fifteen
hundred people down there with no church of any kind. Those people
need a church."

We started by having a Vacation Bible School in the schoolhouse.
My classmates, Brother and Mrs. Case helped in the Kayjay ministry.
Mrs. Case was very good with flannel graph stories. After the Vacation
Bible school a few families wanted to start a church. We got an old
night club that had closed down. We found an old juke box and made
it the pulpit and rolled out bales of hay for the people to sit on. We
started a church.

Brother Case wanted to be the minister of the church in Kayjay.

I got him started but I couldn't stay because I was the pastor of the Concord Church in Flat Lick. He got a big church in Louisville to back him in that work and he stayed there for two years. When we left Kentucky to come back to Tennessee, I recommended him to the church at Flat Lick.

———————————

JOHN J. SMITH

FOUR MILE MINE

THERE WAS A MAN IN THE CHURCH AT FLAT LICK NAMED LAWSON. HE and his wife had five children. They lived at the foot of the hill below the church. Every Sunday morning they filled the second pew. He worked in the Four Mile mine.

When they went back to work after the 1945 Christmas holidays there was a tremendous explosion. He was one of the miners trapped in the mine. The news went out nationwide. "Twenty seven men trapped in a burning mine 2 1/4 miles deep under a mountain."

The explosion released a lot of methane gas. To keep the gas from getting to them they sealed themselves off in a side tunnel. They had been taught to find a short, blind end tunnel and built a wall of rocks and coal and mud. The rescue team found a message on the wall in the main tunnel; "SEVEN MEN TRAPPED ALIVE". The miners drew an arrow to where they were and got behind the wall and sealed it up. Those seven men were found alive and brought out. Mr. Lawson was not in that group.

They were in the mine several days before they were found. In order to save as much oxygen as possible they laid on the cold floor. They never recovered from their ordeal. They were all dead within a few years.

As long as the rescue effort lasted, the families and friends of the trapped men gathered at the front of the mine. They waited night and day. I got permission from the National Guard to go down through that great army of people to try to comfort the families. There wasn't anything a person could do if you were not on one of the rescue teams. They just stood around in the rain and the snow. People came in from Washington DC and mine rescue specialists came from all parts of the nation.

Mr. Lawson's father was there waiting for any word about his son. He had been there for thirty six straight hours. I tried to get him to go home and get some sleep and a hot bath. He just stood there and stared at the opening to the mine. The weather was terrible. It snowed and sleeted and rained but he would not move. He had a big black hat that kept the rain off his face but the water ran along the brim and down his back. He was wet and cold. I touched him on the shoulder and said, "Mr. Lawson your family sent me to get you to come home for a while." He just shook his head. He wouldn't look at me. I stepped around so he would have to look at me. I said, "Mr. Lawson, I got permission to come in here and take you home. I will bring you back."

He still wouldn't look at me. His lips began to quiver and big tears ran down his dirty unshaven face. He said, "Preacher, my boy is in that mine and it is on fire. I don't want anything to eat; I don't want to sleep; I don't want dry clothes; I just want my boy out of that mine. I'm going to stay here to see if he is going to get out." I was defeated. I had to turn and walk away because he was determined to stay.

His son was not one of the miners who were found alive. In fact it was several years before they got some of the bodies out. After they did every thing they could do, they sealed up the mine so it could burn its self out. They plugged up all the tunnels and poured concrete in the vent shafts.

The explosion was so powerful it blew timbers out of the mouth of the mine. The problem was not that the mine had collapsed. The problem was that the mine caught fire. The coal was burning. They not only had to put the fire out, they had to rebuild the timber support system as they went.

When they found Mr. Lawson, he was sitting against the wall as if he was taking a nap. If the methane gas had not got him the fire used up all the oxygen and he suffocated.

It was one of the most heart rendering scenes I ever saw. The whole valley was full of people milling around in the cold rain. There were flood lights at the front of the mouth of the mine and every time a rescue party came out the crowd would surge forward to see if they had found any of the men. Many of the rescue workers got hurt or overcome with smoke. I talked to two men who were carrying one of their co-workers out on a stretcher. They were dressed in asbestos suits, high top gloves and face masks. I said, "What is it like in there?" One of them said, "It's like Hell in there preacher, it's like Hell."

I got to turning that over in my mind. I guess it was like Hell. The coal was on fire and they couldn't put it out and the trapped men were on the other side of the fire. Then I said to myself, "No, no, it's not like hell." Seven of those 27 men were brought out alive. I was standing there when they brought them out. Hell is a one way street. No man can ever come back form Hell." After that, I had a deeper compassion for the unsaved.

———————————

JOHN J. SMITH

CUBAGE

HALF WAY BETWEEN HARLAN AND PINEVILLE, KENTUCKY THE ROAD to Cubage turns off the highway. It goes east toward the mountain range that separates Kentucky from Virginia. In 1946 there was no bridge over the Cumberland River, so the road to Cubage was located at a place where you could ford the river. If the river was low it was not difficult to ford and drive all the way to Cubage but if the river was up, the only way to get to Cubage was to walk across a swinging footbridge and hike about seven miles into the valley.

The road followed a creek bed into a large basin shaped valley. The road was as much in the creek as it was alongside the creek. Every time we crossed the creek it was an adventure. The road had been there a long time. In some places, wagon wheels had worn deep grooves in the rock roadbed. Thousands of wagon loads of virgin timber had been brought out of that valley. Saw milling and a few truck mines were still the primary industry in the valley. Some veins of coal were too small to justify the construction of a railroad. The coal was brought out and loaded into trucks.

One of the ministries of Clear Creek Mountain Preachers School was to conduct Vacation Bible Schools in areas where there were no churches. My father went to Cubage to conduct a Vacation Bible School. I went with him. I took my trumpet and helped with the music. I blew bugle calls to signal the time to change activities and I helped the boys with their crafts.

Most days we could ford the river and drive all the way into Cubage but one day, after a heavy rain, we came to a place where we could not ford the creek. We parked the car and walked the rest of the way in.

Cubage was an interesting community. At one time it was a significant settlement but both the highway and the railroad had passed it by. In 1946, it was isolated from the normal pace of life in Bell County. There was a two story brick school house, a general store and a post office that spoke of a more significant past. Scattered around the valley were quite a few small houses. There were still several subsistence farms.

In the early part of the nineteenth century, the original settlers were farmers who came into the valley through the Cumberland Gap. The farmers built their houses at the head of a small branch and the saw millers and miners took the land on the sides of the hills. The area was still so isolated that the mail was delivered on mule back.

The day we had to walk in, we came to a little cabin up on the side of the mountain. There were two scraggly looking children playing on the front porch. Dad went into the yard to talk to them.

Dad said, "We are having a Vacation Bible School at the schoolhouse. Would you like to come and see what we are doing?"

The boy said, "I ain't never heard of one."

Dad said, "We have lots of fun; we play games and tell Bible stories and sing songs. You do know how to sing songs, don't you?"

He said, "Nope."

Dad said, "Don't you know how to sing, 'Oh, how I love Jesus?'"

He said, "Nope."

Dad said, "Surely you know, 'Jesus loves me this I know.'"

He said, "Nope."

Dad said, "Do you know any songs?"

He said, "One."

Dad said, "What is it?"

He said, "In the pines, in the pines where the sun never shines and you shiver when the cold wind blows."

By the end of the week my daddy had taught those children and about 40 other children to sing,

> 'Oh, how I love Jesus'
> > and
> 'Jesus loves me this I know'
> > and
> a whole bunch of courses like,
> 'The B I B L E that's the book for me'
> > and

'This little light of mine, I'm go'n let it shine'
    and
'Every day with Jesus is sweeter than the day before'
    and
a dozen others.

    Today there is an excellent highway through Cubage. In fact, the road is so good you can pass right through Cubage and never know it. I'm sure that if you took enough time to stop and talk to enough people you would find a few who would say, "Back in the late forties a preacher came in here and held a Vacation Bible School. He told me about Jesus and I have been a Christian ever since."

*"And when he sowed, some seeds … fell into good ground
and brought forth fruit …"*
Matthew 13:4 & 8

ANDREW SMITH

THE FLAT LICK REVIVAL

In 1943 my father was the pastor of the Concord Baptist Church in Flat Lick, Kentucky. Flat Lick is just north of Pineville, Kentucky in the heart of the coal mining district of eastern Kentucky. The church building was built of stone and was the coldest building I ever experienced.

My father was the pastor for about 2 years and then moved to Tennessee. About 2 ½ years later he got a call from the chairman of the deacons asking him to come back and preach a revival.

They started the revival on Sunday morning and there was a nice crowd. That night there was an even larger crowd. Monday night the people came but nothing was happening. Something was wrong. He could feel it in his soul. Tuesday afternoon he called the deacons he knew and asked them to meet him early before the services for a prayer meeting. He said, "Men there is something wrong here. I can feel it in my heart and I am not going back out there to that pulpit until I have peace in my heart. I have to have the power of the Holy Spirit with me." They began to pray and it came time to start the service.

My father said, "I am not ready yet, you go on out there and start the singing." They sang the usual number of songs but may father was still back in the little room behind the piano praying. So they sang a few more songs until he came out and began to preach. As he began to preach he saw the pastor and his wife come in the back door. He said that he never preached with more power in his entire life. The Spirit began to move the people and decisions began to be made for the Lord.

By Thursday night the house was not only full but there were people standing up all around the walls. By the time the revival was over there had been 43 decisions; 37 by profession of faith. It was the greatest revival the church had ever seen.

On Sunday afternoon, as he was getting ready to go back to Georgia the pastor came to him and said, "I have something I've got to talk to you about." My father said, "Well what is it you need to say?" The pastor said, "I didn't want you up here. I resented your coming.

All I could hear was, 'Just wait until Brother Smith gets here, then we will hear some preaching' or 'Brother John will set them straight.' It was, 'Brother Smith this and Brother Smith that until I was so sick of hearing about you I could die.'" By Tuesday afternoon I was so miserable I went home from work early and told my wife to send the children out into the yard to play because we were going to get on our knees and pray until the burden was lifted. Services had already started by the time we got the victory. That was the reason we came in late."

My father said, "Glory be, you got the victory and I got the power at exactly the same time!"

ANDREW SMITH

CAMP PATTERSON

In 1946 John J. Smith gradated from the Clear Creek Mountain Preachers' Bible School and moved his family to a little yellow house on East Brainerd Road in the eastern suburbs of Chattanooga, Tennessee.

He preached a few revivals and supplied in several churches in the area. He thought for a few months that the Lord might be calling him into the evangelistic ministry because he was successful in revivals in small churches in Kentucky, Tennessee and Georgia. He said that he knew that he was not Billy Graham but maybe God needed a preacher who could relate to small country churches.

That all changed one Saturday morning when he went to Ringgold, Georgia to get a hair cut. He sat down in Buck Buchanan's chair and Buck asked him where he was preaching. He said that he was not preaching anywhere. Buck said, "Why don't you come down to Poplar Springs tomorrow and preach for us?"

That began almost three years of work at Poplar Springs Baptist Church. The attendance increased from 25 to 84 in Sunday School and he baptized 45 converts. They built and paid for a new stone worship center.

His vision, however, was larger. He began to teach the Bible in the schools. At one time he was teaching 1500 children a week. His work with children was the reason the Lord laid upon his heart the dream to build a Children's Bible Camp. He knew if he could establish a camp he would be able to reach many children who would never attend a regular Sunday School.

He didn't have any money. He didn't have any resources. He didn't have any support but he had a dream. He was never afraid to dream the impossible dream. He began to look for a piece of property that had a stream that could be used as a swimming pool and wooded hills where he could build cabins.

One afternoon during a missions conference he took one of the speakers, Dr. A. Scott Patterson, a retired missionary to Nigeria, to see the old Bruce Robertson farm in Boynton, Georgia. He said, "Dr.

Pat, do you think I could build a camp for children on this farm"? Dr. Patterson said, "You can do anything, Brother Smith, that you want to do, if it is the Lord's will, if you have the strength to work, the faith to pray and the patience to wait upon the Lord." He took a ten dollar bill out of his billfold and made the first donation to what was eventually named the 'A. Scott Patterson Camp for Children'.

We moved to the old farm house in January 1948. The house had no running water, no electricity and no toilet of any kind. There was no insulation in the walls, the floor or the roof. The only source of heat was a wood burning stove and a fireplace. Those were tough times.

He arranged for electrical power and wired the house for lights and power. We dug a ditch and laid a water line 1/3 mile through the woods. We put in a bathroom and a water heater. It never was a modern house but it was livable and it was on the property where the camp would be built.

Work started on the camp in the spring of 1948. Most of the work was by volunteer labor and a lot of that labor was by John Smith, his two boys and their friend Paul Atchley. The mill trace was cleaned out, the mill pond was repaired, the blackberry vines and honeysuckle thickets were cleaned away. Cabins were built on the side of the hill. His brother Emmitt cut pine trees off the homeplace and sent a truckload of lumber. Churches donated concrete blocks and kegs of nails. On July 5th, 33 boys arrived for the first camp. Dr. Patterson came and pitched a tent under a big sycamore tree and told children about missions in Nigeria. Only God knows how many children gave their hearts to Jesus at Camp Patterson.

After the construction of the first buildings, Ruben Brock, one of the deacons at Poplar Springs, came over to see the camp. He said. "Brother John, you could see all of this when it was still a briar patch couldn't you?" Ruben was right: John Smith could see what normal men could not see. He was determined to be totally dedicated to the will of God. He was pressing toward the mark of the high calling and his dreams had no limit.

ANDREW SMITH

CALIFORNIA

IN 1950, MY FATHER BORROWED A TENT FROM A LARGE CHURCH IN Chattanooga and preached a revival in Burning Bush, a community in Catoosa County, Georgia. .

After the revival, several men came to him and asked him if he would bring his tent to a suburb of Chattanooga. When that revival concluded ten men pledged their support if he would help them start a new church.

The intersection of East Brainard Road and Graysville Road was about 5 miles from two Baptist Churches. Morris Hill Baptist was an old established church that ministered to the residual Baptist in the area and Concord Baptist was a newer suburban church that ministered to the middle class professional residents. There was a need for a third church to minister to the blue collar residents. The church that John and his ten friends established filled that need.

They built the facilities in phases over a period of 7 years. First was a ground floor room with a temporary roof and a sawdust floor. Later, they built a sanctuary and a Sunday School wing. He worked with complete dedication and developed a strong missions minded church.

He also built a home on Julian Road. The back lot line of the church property and the back lot line of their new house aligned. My mother was once again in a new house.

In 1956 a missionary from Kern County, California named John Heard presented at a World Missions conference in Chattanooga. He told about the need for pastors to start new churches in California. Mr. Heard asked dad to come to California and preach a series of revivals. He discovered a need in California that to him was a call like the call from Macedonia to the Apostle Paul

When he came home he said, "Gertie, God is calling us to a small mission in California." She said, "John, are you sure?" He replied, "Gertie, we have always wanted to be foreign missionaries but we don't have enough education. I am convinced there are more lost people in

California than there are in some foreign countries." A week later they were gone!

They loaned, gave away or sold their furniture, stored, trashed or burned the papers and the 25 years of junk they couldn't pack into the trunk and the back seat of a 1956 Plymouth and headed west.

She said good bye to her aged and senile mother, her brothers and sisters, her eldest son and his family, her middle child and his new bride, her pregnant daughter and her husband and perhaps the most painful of all, her only grandchild.

She didn't realize that she was a living example of Matthew 19:29 but she did know how to sing, "Wherever He Leads I'll Go."

> *"And everyone that hath forsaken houses, or brethren, or*
> *sisters, or father, or mother, or wife, or children, or lands,*
> *for my name's sake ... shall inherit everlasting life."*
> Matthew 19:29

I stood and wept as I watched the Plymouth start the trip to California.

It was not easy for him to leave a church he had nurtured from its very infancy. It wasn't easy for my mother leave her new home, her children and grandchild. But, it was not the first time she had moved when her husband heard a call from God. In January 1958 he went to California to accept the pastorate of a new church that was meeting in an old night club. They stayed in California 10 years.

A normal man would have been content to be the pastor of a good suburban church like East Brainard but John Smith was not a normal man. He was a man dedicated to the will of God and he was pressing toward the mark of the high calling.

He was the pastor of three churches while he was in California; Stockdale Baptist Church, The First Baptist Church of Lamont and Panama Baptist Church.

The Stockdale Church grew from 27 people to a congregation that could build a new sanctuary and a Sunday School building. When I visited them in 1960 they had just finished and occupied the building.

The city of Bakersfield had been struck with an earthquake a few years earlier. The city passed new ordinances that required buildings to be constructed to withstand seismic forces. .

The Building Department of the City of Bakersfield had never dealt with a person like John Smith. He thought he could build like he did in Tennessee and Georgia. He did not know about construction documents signed and sealed by an architect and a signed construction contract with a general contractor. He simply ordered stock plans from the Sunday School Board and arranged with somebody to pour the foundation. The men of the church bought lumber and began to erect walls. The building department was flabbergasted. They had never dealt with a church that wanted to build its own building. Eventually there was a compromise between the city and the church. The city spent a lot more time inspecting the construction than they normally did. The church had to deal with a lot more regulations than they thought possible.

John had been a builder before he was a preacher. He built three houses in Ohio, he led the church at Flat Lick to remodel the basement into classrooms, he led the church at Poplar Springs to build a new stone auditorium and he led the church at East Brainard through three building programs. All of these efforts were essentially pay as you go programs. Seldom did they borrow money and if they did they paid it back within a year or two.

The work at First Baptist Lamont was almost an interlude. Lamont was an established church and there was not a significant challenge. John Smith was a man who thrived on challenge.

The Panama work started when he found a little white church building, about seven miles south of Bakersfield, California, that had been abandoned by the Presbyterians, the Methodist and the Congregationalist. He asked some of his friends to help him clean up the building. He preached a revival. The first night two people came forward to join the church. They were John and Gertrude Smith. By the end of the week there were eight members and John Smith was involved in another impossible dream.

He was the pastor of Panama Baptist Church for four years. He baptized 56 people and the attendance grew to over a hundred people. Twenty years later the church had over 400 members.

ANDREW

THE CELEBRATION

April 26, 1996

FIFTY YEARS AGO, JOHN J. SMITH WALKED FORWARD TO SHAKE THE hand of Dr. L. C. Kelly and receive his certificate from Clear Creek Mountain Preachers School. He was one of four to graduate that day. They were the first men to finish the three year course at Clear Creek. It was a significant day in 1946 when the first class of full time students graduated

Dr. Kelly started a summer school for mountain preachers in 1923 and many young men and many churches in the Appalachian Mountain region of Kentucky, Tennessee and Virginia benefited from his vision.

Dr. Bill Whitiker who is now president of the school called about a year ago to ask about dad. I told him that dad had died in 1993. He said that the school was planning a 50 year celebration of the first graduates and asked if I would attend and represent my father. I felt greatly honored.

Dr. Tim Searcy, who is associate Professor of Pastoral Ministries at Clear Creek Baptist Bible College, called about a month ago to see if I was planning to attend the celebration. At the time we were waiting for mother's death so I delayed my decision until after her funeral. I then made arrangements for a day off and called to tell him I would be happy to be there.

I had visited the campus previously so I was not totally surprised by the changes but I still instinctively went to Kelly Hall and went up to the chapel on the second floor. When I opened the door and saw exercise equipment I knew I was in the wrong place. I heard some women talking and could smell food cooking in the kitchen so I asked them where I could find the Chapel. The school had built an administration, classroom, library, chapel building several years ago.

I was early so I spent the next 30 minutes looking at the old photographs and meeting several officials of the school. The corridor was lined with photographs of all 50 classes. The first was of five men standing in the yard in front of Kelly Hall. They were John Stringer, Wallace Starr, John Smith, Lewis Searcy and Calvin Fuson. Wallace Starr was in the picture but he apparently did not finish his courses in time to be in the first graduating class.

The chapel service was as much to impart a little history and heritage to the current students as it was to honor the first class. There were two family members present from the first class, Tim Searcy and me. I was the only person present who attended the first graduation. Tim was born after his father graduated. Dr. Aldridge, who was the speaker at the celebration, arrived on the Clear Creek Campus on April 27, 1946 the day after the first class graduated He taught at the school for several years and was later (1954-1982) president of the school.

After the service we went to Kelly Hall for a nice lunch. I ate with Creed Caldwell who now teaches at Clear Creek. He was a teenager when his father attended the school in the 1950's. He and I had similar experiences such as swimming in the "Big Rock" swimming hole and exploring all the trails through the mountains.

I thought the entire event was well planned and carried out. The school still fills a vital need for the education of preachers and church professionals who are called to minister in the mountain areas of Kentucky, Tennessee and Virginia. Graduates of the school are now found in many states and in several foreign countries. The school has changed over the years. It is now an accredited Bible College but it is still contending with a strong anti-education element among mountain preachers. The proud tradition of solid, conservative Christian education that Dr. Kelly started over 75 years ago is stronger than ever at Clear Creek Baptist Bible College.

ANDREW SMITH

RETIREMENT

WHEN DAD WAS 60 YEARS OLD HE BEGAN TO THINK ABOUT COMING home. His success in California brought him to the attention of the Tennessee Baptist Convention. They asked him to be the Director of Missions for the Union Baptist Association in White County, Tennessee. White County is about 70 miles east of Nashville and on the western edge of the Cumberland Plateau. There he met a new challenge. There were churches in those mountains that had been feuding since before the Civil War and there were pastors with visions so narrow they hardly knew what the word missions meant.

That didn't scare John Smith. He knew that if it was the Lord's will and that if he would work and pray the results would come. He not only got the churches to cooperate, he led them to support missions and expanded their vision to see beyond the hills of the Cumberland Plateau.

He did something that was radical in that part of the country. He organized a Vacation Bible School in the black community. It was so successful that a preacher came up from McMinnville and reconstituted the black Baptist Church in Sparta, Tennessee.

When it came time to take children to summer camp he took some of the black children. That was not a popular thing to do. There was a lot of protest but he told them that God loved black children in Tennessee just like he loved black children in Africa and that if they wanted to come to camp he was going to let them come.

Tennessee State Baptist had a 65 year old mandatory retirement rule so he sold his home in Sparta and took a vacation to Florida.

Before he got back home he received a call from Salem Baptist Church in Catoosa County Georgia. He enjoyed that pastorate and made many friends but he needed more of a challenge.

He answered a call to be the pastor of Cedar Springs Baptist Church which is about 8 miles east of Cleveland, Tennessee. His work there was rewarding. They bought a bus and began to bring in many children who would have otherwise had no opportunity to go to Sunday School. The church built a cabin at the associational camp where they had many retreats for both youth and adults

During the years they were at Cedar Springs they began to talk about where they wanted to live after they retired. He talked to me about it many times. His line always went, "What do you think about ... ...?" He never, for a second considered going to a "retirement village" or a "retirement home" and he never considered retiring to Florida. It was always, "Build a little house." One weekend I went to see them and he said, "I've bought a place where we can retire."

He said, "Our friends, the Robertsons from California, came to visit us. We took them to dinner in Chattanooga. We were on our way back to Cleveland when your mother said, 'John, let's take them over to East Brainerd and show them the house we owned on Julian Road?'" When we got to the house there was a "For Sale" sign in the yard."

Later he said, "Gertie, how would you like to retire in the house on Julian Road?" She said, "I always liked living in that house. I'd just as soon live there as anywhere."

He called the real estate company. They were asking $33,000.00 for the house. He was disappointed because he simply was not going to pay $33,000.00 for a house he built for $11,000.00. He told my mother that they would just have to find something else.

A week or two later he was in the supermarket buying a few groceries. He said he picked up a pound of coffee to put in the basket. When he checked the price it was $3.50. It hit him like a thunderbolt. "I could have bought that pound of coffee for 50 cents in 1954." He left the cart half full of groceries right there in the middle of the aisle and went home. He said, "Gertie, if you want that house I will buy it for you."

He bought the house; gave them $12.000.00 in cash and took out a 30 year loan on the remainder. He was 70 years old at the time."

When he was 71 years old, he retired a second time. He was loading the rental truck when the chairman of the pulpit committee from Benton Station Baptist Church got out of his car ... He said, "Would you come up and preach for us for a while?" He said the committee was looking for a young preacher who could relate well with the young people but they needed somebody to help them for a few weeks..

Four weeks later the committee asked him if he would be their pastor. He said, "I thought you were looking for a young preacher." They said, "You might not be young but you relate to our young people better than any pastor we have ever had and you are the best preacher we have ever heard." He stayed four years

He was never satisfied with simply doing what was expected of him. While he was at Benton Station he was also the moderator of the Polk County Baptist association, the Chairman of Evangelism and the Director of the Camp.

While at Benton Station John and Gertrude celebrated their 50th wedding anniversary. The event was attended by children, grand children, great grand children, nieces, nephews, brothers and sisters, cousins and many friends. He said that the celebration made up for what they did not have on their wedding day. What they did have at their wedding was a man who packed a lunch for his bride and walked her down to a spring underneath some big pine trees and sang to her, "When your hair has turned to Silver I will Love you Just the Same."

In October 1982 he retired again. It wasn't long before he was the interim pastor at Mount Vernon Baptist Church Sales Creek. He had served as interim pastor at the church 37 years ago.

The next summer they responded to a call from the Home Missions Board to be the summer minister at Boyne City Baptist Chapel in Northern Michigan.

His last professional ministry was as the Associate Pastor for the First Baptist Church of Apison, Tennessee. He liked to talk about the old people in the church. At least half of them were younger than he was. He visited with them in their homes and ministered to them when they were in the hospital. He taught a Sunday School class he called the "Rainbow Class" because it was open to all comers. He taught men and women, young and old, married and single, agile and handicapped. All kinds of people wanted to be in "Uncle Johnny's class". He filled in for the pastor and had a very fruitful four years as Associate Pastor.

The fourth time he retired he was 82 years old. He had broken both hips and as he said, "This old Parkinson's disease is slowing me dow.n.

When they gave up housekeeping and moved in with my sister in Chamblee, Georgia they said that they wanted to join Andy's Church. One of their proudest moments was when they stepped out and walked down the aisle to join Dunwoody Baptist Church; the church that I had served as pastor 30 years previously..

The last time he spoke from the pulpit I stood beside him to steady him. He related how God had used him as a servant in the Kingdom. He said,

> "Dwight L. Moody used to say, 'It remains yet to be seen what can be done with a life turned completely over to God'. When I answered the call to preach I said, 'With God's help I will be that man'. I have tried to be that man for over forty years. Now I can say with the Apostle Paul, 'I have pressed toward the mark for

the prize of the high calling of God in Jesus Christ;
and, 'I have fought the good fight, I have finished my
course, I have kept the faith' ."

Andrew Smith

SECTION TWO

In June of 1950, four days after I graduated from high school, I left home and went away to college. I only had resources to complete one semester of college . By early 1951 the Korean conflict was at its most desperate phase and I knew that an eighteen year old with no job and no deferment would not remain a civilian very long. I joined the Navy. Four years in the Navy and then five years in collage brought many changes in my life. These stories are from the years 1950 to 1961.

1. GOING TO COLLAGE
2. GEORGIA TECH
3. CLAIRMONT BAPTIST CHURCH
4. BUFORD HIGHWAY BAPTIST CHURCH
5. YORUBA
6. DUNWOODY
7. HOSPILITY
8. SLEEPING DEACONS
9. ORDINATION
10. THE CAT
11. THE FUNERAL
12. THE GENESIS OF A NEW CHURCH IN DUNWOODY

GOING TO COLLEGE

I T IS AMAZING THAT AFTER A LIFETIME OF CONVERSATIONS, IN WHICH a person may speak and hear billions of words, your mind can go back 70 years and remember one poignant sentence.

One of the things I inherited from my father is the need to plan ahead. It is a little more dramatic than that, because he and I both have a tendency to dream the impossible dream. The impossible dream when I was a senior in high school was to go to college. My family had no money for college. There was barely enough money to buy books for high school. Dad made less than 50 dollars a week.

That didn't keep me from dreaming about going to college. My father taught me to dream and my mother had always encouraged me, "Be somebody." She had a fierce sense of self worth. She had from the time I can remember made statements like, "You are as good as anybody" or "You can be whatever you want to be."

Dad had also set a powerful example by going back to school when he was 35 years old. He finished the ninth grade and like many other young men in the south, went north to find work, He worked on the assembly line of the Chevrolet plant in Cincinnati, Ohio. After he answered the call to the ministry, he went back to school. He finished three years of Bible School and one year of college. I didn't know how I was going to do it but I knew that somehow I was going to go to college.

One Sunday afternoon during my senior year my father asked me to go for a drive. Going for a drive was a device he used when he wanted to talk to me. I suppose it is a symbol of our culture that many of the most important conversations of our lives occur in an automobile. In the past, the woodshed or the barn or the "back forty" was the place for serious conversations. The woodshed and the barn are gone from most of our lives. In 1950. the car was the place for serious conversations.

We were driving down a country road when dad pulled over to the side of the road and stopped the car. I knew that he had something serious to say when he stopped the car. Had it been something casual he would have talked while he was driving. He said. "I know you want to go to college and I want you to have the best education you can possibly have." He paused and swallowed hard and said, "You know we don't have any money, but," and he choked up and big tears rolled down his cheeks, "I'll pray for you every day."

It took ten years, from 1950 to 1960 for those prayers to be answered, but they were a constant source of strength. The memory of that sentence, that probably took a little more that a second to speak, was indelibly etched in my mind.

The fact that I did not have any money did not prevent me from looking for a way to go to college. I had heard about Berry College in North Georgia and Berea College in Eastern Kentucky where a student could work for tuition. I went to one of my teachers and asked how I could get information about those colleges.

The teacher was a young red headed woman who taught chemistry. She probably wasn't more that 5 or 6 years older than her students. She was a new teacher and interested in her students. I think she was the only teacher I ever had who did such things as have a bunch of students over to her apartment. She and her husband had gone to a small college in the northern part of Tennessee called Lincoln Memorial University. She said that LMU sill had a few work scholarships.

She gave me a catalogue and I wrote the school and asked if they had any work scholarships. They wrote back that they had a summer project that could still use a few workers. They didn't promise a job during the regular school year, but I could work full time during the summer. I decided to take the offer. I went to work four days after I graduated from high school.

I told dad I would take the bus to LMU. I knew that his old car was not able to make the trip. He wanted to do what he could do to help me. He borrowed a car so he could take me to the college and get me settled in. I do not remember who loaned him the car but I remember that it was a new 1950 Dodge.

Later, after going to school at Georgia Tech and working 5 years as the staff architect for The University of Tennessee, the LMU campus seems very small. But, when we drove up to the front gate in June of 1950, it looked enormous. I was glad he was there to ask the right questions and find the Dean of Admissions and get me settled into my room. I was glad that he had not listened to my brave statements about doing it on my own. I am sure I could have done it somehow but barging into a new situation never was my long suite. He knew me well enough to know the kind of help I needed and the kind of help he was able to give.

I have found that prayer and someone to go with you when you are entering new and unfamiliar territory is more valuable than money. In countless times, when decisions had to be made, or I faced what seemed to be insurmountable difficulties, I would hear my father say "I'll pray for you every day."

GEORGIA TECH

EVER SINCE MY SENIOR YEAR IN HIGH SCHOOL, I HAD PLANNED TO study medicine and become a doctor. I had good grades in biology and chemistry and I had always wanted to be a person who helped others.

When I joined the Navy I asked to be assigned to the Hospital Corps so I could get experience in medicine. In the summer of 1951 the Korean War was at its most intense so there was no trouble getting into the Hospital Corps. In fact many recruits were assigned to the Hospital Corps who had no desire whatever to be in medical work. I finished Hospital Corps School and was sent to Corpus Christie Naval Hospital. After about 6 months as a general purpose corpsman I applied for Operating Room Technician School. After completing training in the school I was transferred to Portsmouth Naval Hospital.

I learned a lot. In time I was the senior enlisted man on the operating room staff. I scrubbed on many operations. There were times when I was called out in the middle of the night for an emergency appendectomy and I knew more about the procedure than the young intern doing the operation. By the time my enlistment was over I had assisted in hundreds of operations.

One thing I discovered was that it takes a long time to become a surgeon. Very few pre-med freshmen have any idea what is required to be a doctor. That is true for most young people starting their education. Few freshmen have a good understanding of the profession they have chosen.

I learned that it took four years of pre-med, four years of medical school, one year as an intern and four to five years as a resident. I was naive enough to think that I could go through all of that with a wife but I knew that I could never do it with a family. When I found out that we were going to have a baby, I began to think about other professions.

I considered all of the other things I loved to do. I had helped my father and my uncles with their building projects on the farm. I also had some artistic talent, a good sense of proportion and scale. After a lot of thought I decided that I should consider architecture. The five years required for a Bachelor of Architecture looked a lot more achievable than eight years to get an MD.

I knew that Georgia Tech had an excellent College of Architecture. I began to make plans to enroll at Georgia Tech.

When Mary Jo and I married, my mother and father lived in Boynton, a small village in Catoosa County, Georgia. Not long after we married dad started a new church in East Brainerd, which is a suburb of Chattanooga, Tennessee. East Brainerd and Boynton are only about five miles apart but one is in Georgia and the other is in Tennessee.

When I found out that mom and dad were going to move to Tennessee, I deliberately did not change my home address with the personnel department at the base. I was discharged back to the address in Boynton, Georgia.

When Mary Jo and Karen and I came home from the Navy we spent a night or two with mom and dad and then went to Atlanta to find an apartment. I can not remember how we ended up with the apartment off of Ashford Dunwoody road.

It is interesting what you remember and what you forget. For example, I have no idea how we got our furniture from Chattanooga to Atlanta. We didn't have a lot of furniture but there was more than would fit in our car.

When I was discharged, the Navy shipped our furniture back home. We kept the barrel that the dishes were shipped in and used it as the base for a kitchen table. I bought a used door for the table top and we used the crates as our kitchen chairs. We made the decision to rent an unfinished apartment . We had a baby bed for Karen and a mattress on the floor in our bedroom. We paid my mother's Uncle Charlie $15.00 for a chair. We sat a table lamp on a crate by the chair. That was our living room furniture.

Mary Jo likes to tell the story about a preacher coming to visit. We only had one chair. She was embarrassed but insisted that he sit in the chair while she stood and talked with him.

My grades in high school algebra were not very good. Those grades and the fact that it had been 4 years since I graduated from high school forced me to take four remedial courses before I could enroll in Georgia Tech. I made good grades in English, Physics, Algebra I and Algebra II in night school and was accepted as a full time student for the fall quarter of 1955.

That was a high water mark for me. The whole four years in the Navy were preliminary to the start of my college studies. I filled out all the papers with the VA and was approved to start getting money from the GI bill.

The big surprise came when I went to pay my fees. After waiting in a long line I finally got to the pay window and the clerk found my papers and asked for several hundred dollars. I don't remember exactly how much it was but it was a lot more than what I expected and several times as much as what I had.

I told them that there had to be some mistake. They said that all they wanted was the standard fee for "Out of State" tuition. I was much relieved. I told them that I had been a Georgia resident for eight years.

The clerk sent me to see one of the registers. He said, "Son, your application says that your father lives at 1054 Julian Road in Chattanooga, Tennessee. That makes you a Tennessee resident. You will have to pay out of state tuition." I told him that I had not lived in Tennessee since 1947 but he said that it was my father's address that established residency.

I explained that I lived in Georgia when I joined the Navy and that when I was discharged I moved immediately back to Georgia. Besides that I was over 21 years old, married and had been on my own since I was 17 years old. He said that none of that made any difference. The rules of Georgia Tech were that residency was set by where the parents lived. He went on to explain that they had to have strict rules about residency because many out of state students wanted to go to Georgia Tech. They would do all kinds of things to establish Georgia residency. To counteract that, they had set residency by the address of the parents.

I thought I would die. I couldn't believe it. How was I going to tell Mary Jo that all our dreams of going to Georgia Tech to study architecture were down the tube? There was no way I could pay the out of state tuition. I could barely pay the in-state fees.

I kept thinking. There had to be a way to work it out. It was not fair. I understood why they had the rules but my case was different. I was no more a Tennessee resident than Genghis Kahn! I asked if I could wait a year and then reapply. He said that that would not be accepted because once residency was established it could never be changed.

After a while, probably to simply get rid of me, he suggested that I should see if the University of Tennessee would accept me as a Tennessee resident. "If Tennessee will not accept you, I will reconsider your case."

I was somewhat relieved but not much. I was relieved because I thought surely Tennessee will not accept me simply because my parents live in the state. I was also distressed because I knew that Tennessee did not have a school of architecture. My choice of architecture was firm. I had not even considered that I might have to study something else.

The next day I hit the road hitchhiking to Knoxville. I didn't have enough money for gas or for bus fare. Why, I didn't try to work it out on the telephone, I don't know. I got to Knoxville before noon and went straight to the registrar's office.

They were very nice to me. I told him my story and the register said, "You say your father lives in Chattanooga?" I said, "Yes" and he said that he would be happy to enroll me as a Tennessee resident; what did I want to study? I told him that I wanted to be an architect and he said that Tennessee did not have an architecture program but I could enroll in the college of Engineering. I thought to myself "UGH" who would ever want to be an engineer!

He told me that there was one other possibility. There was a bill before the Tennessee State Legislature that would help pay the tuition of Tennessee residents who wanted to study architecture in one of the schools in the surrounding states. In 1955, there were not many schools of architecture in the south. Other than Georgia Tech there were schools at Auburn, Florida and North Carolina and some private schools like Tulane and Miami.

The problem was that the amount of assistance was only $200 per quarter and there was no guarantee that the bill would pass.

When I got back on the road that afternoon I was in one of the most serious depressions of my entire life. I was hungry, had no money, had a tough time getting rides and had a very perplexing problem on my mind. It was so unfair. Georgia Tech had such a large request for admission from out of state students, (especially from northeastern states), that they had to establish very rigid rules.

All the way back to Atlanta my mind was spinning like a top. What was I going to do? How was I going to convince the register that I was a Georgia resident? If I couldn't do it, what were we going to do? We had no contingency plans. How would I get a job to hold us over until we could decide what to do? I had already spent 4 years in the Navy which put me behind other guys starting college. What could I do? That was the most depressing few hours of my entire life.

As I passed through Chatsworth, Georgia I remembered playing basketball against Murray County High School. They were tough. I don't know that we ever beat them. I began to think about those days I lived in Catoosa County.

About the time I reached the intersection US 411 and US 41 it hit me like a thunderbolt. I had registered to vote before I left home for the Navy. (Georgia was at that time the only state that allowed 18 year olds to vote. Georgia legislators said that if a person was old enough to die for his country he was old enough to vote.) I then remembered that I had voted by absentee ballot in the 1952 presidential election. I said to myself, "I'd bet anything that I am a registered voter in Catoosa County, Georgia! That's it! If I am a registered voter, I am a resident of the state and nobody can say that I am not."

The next day I scrapped up enough money to buy gas to get to Ringgold. I marched myself into the Catoosa County courthouse and asked to see the County Court Clerk. She looked up the registered voter's list and said that I was a registered voter. I asked her for a notarized statement. She typed one, sealed it and had it signed by the Tax Commissioner.

BERT WARD
TAX COMMISSIONER
Catoosa County
RINGGOLD, GEORGIA

September 28, 1955

To Whom it May Concern;

I hereby Certify that ANDREW L. Smith is a registered voter of
Boynton District (1555), Catoosa County, Georgia since December 14,
1951, which he was born Feb. 24, 1933 and as of this date is still
a qualified voter of Catoosa County, Georgia.

Signed; *Bert Ward P.C.*

Bert Ward, Tax Commissioner
Catoosa County, Georgia

I took my notarized statement to the register at Georgia Tech. He said that he didn't know how he was going to argue against a notarized statement. I was a registered voter in the State of Georgia. He changed the application form and accepted me as a Georgia resident. He said that it was still a little irregular, and that as far as he knew it had never happened before, but unless there was some complaint from somebody at the state capitol, I would not hear anything else about it. I shook his hand and went out of his office a happy young man.

I really don't know what I would have done if I had not remembered that I was a registered voter in Catoosa County, Georgia. To say the least, our lives would have been different.

CLAIRMONT BAPTIST CHURCH

In April 1955, I was discharged from the US Navy and moved to Atlanta with my wife and daughter to study Architecture at Georgia Tech. My father knew that I had not gone to church often while I was in the navy and he was concerned that I would not attend church regularly in Atlanta. He made it his business to come see how we were doing in our new apartment. He brought some old furniture, some civilian clothes and a much needed bag of groceries. My mother brought a coconut pie and fried chicken.

They had hardly unloaded the car when he said, "Let's see if we can find Dr. Patterson." We found a public pay phone and he looked up Dr. Patterson's number and called him. Dr. Patterson said that he had just started a little mission in Chamblee out on Clairmont Road. He asked my father to come to the mission that very night and bring the message. They were meeting in a little five room house. Between that Wednesday and the next Sunday Dr. Patterson had enlisted me to lead the singing and my wife was in charge of the nursery.

There were several significant laymen in Clairmont Baptist Church. Those men plus Dr. Patterson's example and prodding is what made things happen.

"Doc" Snodgrass was a Bible salesman. He went door to door selling big family Bibles. They were 12" high and 10" wide and 3" thick. He made pretty good living at it. All the time he was selling Bibles he was talking to people about their relationship to God. He was what I call a "classic" personal soul winner. He was a natural. It wasn't anything he had learned at a study course and it wasn't something he did because somebody made him feel guilty about it. It was as natural to him as breathing.

"Doc" had a big, quick smile. It was a little unusual because his right incisor tooth was missing. After I had known him for a while I asked him why he didn't have a bridge put in and fill in his missing tooth. He didn't say anything. He simply reached up and took out his upper plate. I said, "Why in the world don't you have that tooth put back in?" He said. "I really can't explain it but one day that tooth started hurting. It was just as if I had a toothache. I put up with it for a while and then I got out my pliers and pulled it out. I got busy and didn't have it put back in and after a while I got used to the way I looked. It seemed that others accepted me with a missing tooth and eventually it became almost a part of my personality. I don't think I will ever have it fixed."

F. M. Davis was a lay preacher. I have forgotten what he did for a living. He was a big bald headed man and he was very good in the pulpit. He was a much sought after evangelist. He died with cancer not too long after we moved to Knoxville.

Walt Griswell was the song leader. He was a post office worker. He had a good voice and was exactly what the little church needed.

There was a young man whose last name was Fox who went from being a Sunday School teacher to being the pastor of a small church a few years later. Dr. Patterson was involved in the starting of a new church down close to Stone Mountain. Fox became the pastor of that church.

Calvin Abernathy was a young man in the church who was a draftsman for Gulf Oil Company. I remember that he drew the plans for the first little building we built at Clairmont. I helped him with the planning but he did the drawings. His lettering was the best I had ever seen. I was jealous because even though I was a pretty good designer even then I couldn't letter worth a whit.

The other man I remember was named Jones. He was a building contractor. I worked for him in the summer of 1955. We built a church building in Morrow, Georgia. We finished the work a few weeks before school started and he had to lay me off. It was a very difficult lesson for me. I knew why he laid me off. He needed to cut his work force and he knew that I was going to school in a few week so he naturally kept the men who would be able to work all fall. It took a lot of discipline for me to be able to worship with Mr. Jones because I needed the work and we barely had enough to eat. I had to make my head take charge of my feelings. It took a while but after a few months my affection and respect for Mr. Jones was as strong as ever.

One of the reasons that there was such a strong lay movement in that church was that Dr. Patterson didn't ask you if you wanted to do a certain job, he simply asked you to do whatever needed to be done. He would say, "I want you to do this". If you couldn't or wouldn't do it you had to turn him down and that wasn't easy to do because he had such high expectations for you. He made you want to please him.

When we started going to Clairmont Baptist Dr. Pattterson simply assumed that I would do anything and everything he asked me to do. My job was to teach teenage boys. That wasn't something that I wanted to do and I didn't think that I was very good at it but there wasn't anybody else to do it so I was elected.

The first Christmas we lived in Atlanta, the whole family came down from Chattanooga to see us. Mom and dad, my sister Jean and my brother Don. Don drove his new 1954 silver streak Pontiac. I was a little jealous. My mother was an excellent seamstress. She made Mary Jo a suit and Karen a little mauve colored outfit with a coat, leggings and a hat with a feather. Don brought me a shirt and Mary Jo a blouse. Jean and her husband,Benny, brought Karen a rocky horse. The first day Karen had more fun playing with the box than she did with the horse. Later she wore that horse out.

Dr. Patterson stayed at Clairmont about two years. That was long enough for the church to grow strong enough to build a building and call a full time pastor. When Rev. Buren Dowdy came, Dr. Patterson left and went up the road to start another church.

BUFORD HIGHWAY BAPTIST CHURCH

DAD TELLS THE STORY ABOUT COMING TO ATLANTA TO VISIT US. WHILE he was there he went to see Dr. Scott Patterson. Dr. Pat was in the process of leaving Clairmont Baptist to start a new work. Dr. Pat took him to a location about half way between Doraville and Norcross, Georgia. He said, "Look at all those new houses. There are people out there everywhere. There are kids all over the place. We've got to get a church started for these people."

Dr. Patterson started the church in a small house and an old bus. They called it Buford Highway Baptist Church.

He had not been at Buford Highway very long before he called me. He asked me to come up to his home in Norcross. He said that he needed my help in locating a new building. We went over to the site and walked around and talked about where to put the building and the parking.

While we were walking across the property he said, "Why don't you come up here and help me?" I said that I didn't mind helping him but I wasn't sure what I could do. He said, "I want you to do whatever needs to be done. The people in this new church are dedicated and loyal but they do not have a lot of experience. You can teach a Sunday School class and organize the Training Union. You can lead the singing when necessary." He paused and then said, "You might even fill in for me when I get sick. I am getting old and I am crippled and I need somebody to help me that I can depend on."

I became his helper. I don't remember how we did it because Mary Jo and Karen stayed at Clairmont Baptist. We only had one car. We worked out a system where I would drop them off at Clairmont and then go up to Buford Highway. The two churches were not very far apart.

One reason that would work was that Dr. Pat preached exactly 22 minutes. The pastor at Clairmont, Rev. Dowdy, preached considerably longer than that. Dr. Pat kept an old fashioned wind up alarm clock on the pulpit. He contended that if you couldn't say what you needed to say in 20 minutes you were wasting time. I always remembered that.

I did what he asked me to do. I taught boys, was director of the Training Union, read the Scripture, made the announcements, led the singing and did anything else that needed to be done.

We built a small building. The men did a lot of work. I remember lifting the wood trusses by hand. A contractor would have used a small crane or a front end loader. We got a rope, a pulley and about six men hoisted them up.

When Dr. Pat caught the flue, he asked me to take care of the preaching service. I don't remember what I said but I remember that he gave me an unabridged copy of Cruden's concordance. I was hoping he would give me ten dollars. Money was scarce back then but Dr. Pat had a much larger vision than one week's groceries.

I stayed with Dr. Patterson about a year before he sent me to the church in Dunwoody, Georgia.

YORUBA

DR. A. SCOTT PATTERSON WAS COMMISSIONED TO GO TO NIGERIA IN 1916. He was a missionary to the Yoruba tribe in the north central part of that country. He was responsible for starting the Baptist schools in Ogbomosho and for establishing many churches.

In the 1930's, after serving over twenty years in Nigeria, he developed a weakness in his ankles and was sent home. He first had to walk on crutches but later learned to walk with two canes. He was the pastor of several small churches in Georgia even though he had to preach sitting down.

When I knew him in the 1950's he still walked with a cane and wore black high top shoes to support his weak ankles.

In the spring of 1938 a serious yellow fever epidemic broke out in Nigeria. All the Southern Baptist missionaries were affected. Some died and others were sent home because they were sick. Southern Baptists were in danger of losing much of the progress they had made in Nigeria.

There was a lot of concern at the Foreign Mission board in Richmond, Virginia. Yoruba is a difficult language to learn and they did not have young missionaries learning the language. Someone said, "What about Scott Patterson down there in Georgia?" The reply was, "Sure, he knows the language but he is all crippled up and besides that he has four young children. We can't ask him to go back to a yellow fever infested Nigeria." The conclusion was however, that Scott Patterson was the only option Southern Baptists had.

Dr. and Mrs. Patterson prayed about it and decided that he should go and she would stay in the States and look after the children. In 1938 they went to Foreign Missions week at Ridgecrest where Dr. Patterson was recommissioned to go back to Nigeria.

Dr. and Mrs. Patterson were sitting on the platform at Ridgecrest when someone asked her how she could possibly give up her husband to go to a yellow fever infested country and leave her to take care of four small children. She answered by quoting King David,

"I will not make an offering to the Lord my God that costs me nothing."
II Samuel 24:24

Andrew Smith
As told by Dr. A. Scott Patterson in 1957

DUNWOODY

ONE DAY, IN NOVEMBER 1957, DR. PATTERSON SAID, "ANDY, I WANT you to go over to a little church in Dunwoody next Sunday." I asked him what he wanted me to do. He told me that the church did not have a pastor and that I was to conduct Sunday services. I said, "Dr. Pat, you know that I can't preach" and he said, "You don't have to. Just go over there and pray over them, they're dead anyway."

He helped me with an outline for a short sermon and told me to not worry. He said that there would not be more than 15 to 20 people and that they would be happy to hear anything I had to say. He had already sent two of my friends, F. M. Davis and "Doc" Snodgrass and it was my turn. I felt obligated to do my turn although I wasn't very thrilled at having to preach a sermon. He said that the church didn't need a preacher; they needed someone to love them and talk to them.

I went and did my best. He was right. There were about 20 people if you count all the children. I can remember most of them. Mr. and Mrs. Swancy, Steve and Mary Bob Kirby and their six children, Mrs. Lucy Anderson, Kenny and Alvine Anderson, Alvin and Ruby Price, Mrs. Burell, Sanford and Martha Burell and their children, Jane Autry and her girls and a few others. They were kind to me and after the evening service Mr. Swancy, Chairman of the Deacons, asked me to come back the next Sunday. I told them that I would and went back to Dr. Pat for another sermon outline. After the second Sunday he asked me to come back for the third time.

After the morning worship service on the third Sunday Mr. Swancy asked me if I would go with him to visit a few families. The people were happy the church wasn't dead after all. They even said they might come back to the services. I don't remember why I raised the issue unless it was because I could see some potential for the church and that I don't like to do things that are not planned and thought out. As we were driving down Mt. Vernon Road I said, "Mr. Swancy, I don't mind coming over here and doing what I can do; you know by now that I am no preacher, but if you want me, I would like to know that

I am going to be here for a while, we can do some planning." He said they had been thinking about what they were going to do. He called me later in the week and asked if I would stay with them until the next "annual preacher calling" in August.

I found out later that Dr. Patterson had told Mr. Swancy before he sent me over there; "That boy can't preach but that doesn't make any difference. You don't need a preacher and you can't afford a preacher anyway. No matter how bad his sermons are, you ask him back and then ask him back again." I don't know whether Dr. Patterson was prophetic or whether he simply had confidence in me. Perhaps he had simply run out of people to send over to Dunwoody. It doesn't matter; the result was that they said that if we would come and help them we could live in the parsonage and they would give us 15 dollars a week.

I was 24 years old and a student of Architecture at Georgia Tech. Mary Jo, our daughter Karen, and I were living in an old converted army barracks that the school was using as off campus married student housing. The parsonage looked like a palace to us and the 15 dollars a week would certainly buy a few groceries. I'm not sure we ever made any money from the work at Dunwoody because there was never a week I didn't spend extra money for gas or books or paper or something for the church. There were also many weeks when there was not enough money to pay the preacher after all the essential bills were paid.

By January I had established four goals for my work at Dunwoody. The first was to get the church back to what I called a regular "Southern Baptist" church. The minister who preceded me had some ideas and methods that were different from what was the norm for a cooperative Southern Baptist church. His conservatism was as much in methods and procedures as it was in theology. I was told that he did not believe in any type of youth ministry. His concept of conversion was much like the concept practiced in the 19th century. He believed in adult conversion, which meant that he would not consider young people until they were at least 16 years old. There was very little evangelism. It had been many years since there had been a Revival.

There was little if any emphasis in missions. The Women's Missionary Union had been dissolved and the budget did not have any provisions for giving to missions. It took a little persuasion but I convinced them that the grace of God obligated them to share with others. They agreed to send 10% of the offerings to missions. That didn't help their ability to pay the preacher but that didn't matter and the fact was that every time we were concerned about the groceries somebody would show up at the door with a dish of fried chicken or a bowl of beans or whatever they had. We never went hungry.

We organized a Women's Missionary Union and a Brotherhood for the men. We started having Training Union and set up working committees to plan and organize the work of the church. I attended the Deacon's meetings. They were surprised when I did not tell them exactly what to do. It took a little while to get things organized and turned around but not as long as might have been expected. They remembered what they had done in the past.

The second goal was to start an emphasis on youth. We began to have after church fellowships and socials and anything else we could think of that would attract young people. I discovered that it had been many years since there had been a Vacation Bible School. We ordered the literature and began to plan for a Vacation Bible School.

The third goal was to emphasize evangelism. Dad said that I wrote him a letter sometime in February and said that I had been there for three months and had preached everything I knew to preach and nobody had been saved. He said he told my mother that if he could see some tear stains on the letter he would be happy. He wrote back and said for me to just keep on preaching the Word and the harvest would come.

We made plans for a Revival. My friends from Clairmont, F. M. Davis, agreed to be the preacher and Walt Griswell came to be the song leader. We did everything we could think of to promote the Revival. We conducted cottage prayer meetings; we visited all over the community; we put flyers in every mailbox in the area and put up posters on telephone poles. We used all the ways we had ever heard of to challenge the people to attend and to bring their friends. We assigned pews to families and challenged them to pack it with friends and we assigned each church department a night and recognized them on that night. The church house was full every night and on Friday night there were men standing in the back of the auditorium.

The lack of an evangelistic effort for the previous years meant that there was a large group of teenagers ready for someone to encourage them to make their confession of faith. They started coming forward after the first service. By the end of the week several adults had been saved and many others had moved their letters and rededicated their lives to Christ. Clarence Autry who married Jane Anderson came the last night and there was great joy all over the house.

It was a great week. There were 22 professions of faith and a total of 46 additions to the church. Several families who had not attended in a long time became active.

There was a small problem after the Revival because there were several candidates for baptism. I went to Dr. Pat for advice. I told him that the church wanted me to baptize the converts but I was not ordained and I wasn't sure a person who was not ordained should baptize people. He thought for a few second the said "We have a tremendous advantage by being Baptist. A Baptist church is totally independent and can by and large do what it wants to do. If they want you to baptize their children they simply need to have a business meeting and authorize you to baptize and no one can say that they are wrong." We borrowed the baptistery at Clairmont Baptist Church and I baptized 12 people. The first adult I baptized was Clarence Autry who became my best friend.

The other goal I set for my work at Dunwoody was to teach the church how to call a full time, trained pastor. I was convinced that my role was to get the church started back toward being a standard Baptist church and stay long enough for them to get strong financially and call a full time pastor. I also wanted them to give up the old fashioned system of calling a preacher every August. I wanted them to change their thinking from calling a "preacher" every 12 months to extending an indefinite call to a man to be their "pastor." I explained the process of electing a pulpit committee who would establish the criteria by which they would look for a pastor. I taught them how to analyze the church budget and determine how much they could pay a pastor.

After the first pulpit committee meeting they came to me and said they did not want to look for anybody because they had the best pastor they had ever had. I told them no; that was not what the church asked them to do. They were to look for a full time, professionally trained pastor. I was in school to be an architect and I did not feel that I had been called to be a professional minister. I told them that they should proceed with the plan they had worked out.

About a month later they came back and said they had been to hear three preachers and that none of them could preach like the preacher already had. I was pleased that my preaching had improved but I still went through the routine all over again. I told them that the task they had been asked to do was not easy. I suggested they take their time. I assured then that I would stay with them until they found the right man.

I went to talk to Dr. Patterson about it. He said, "They need you and they want you to be their pastor. Perhaps you should listen to them.. I said, "But I am going to school to be an architect." He was very firm in his reply, "Don't quit going to school. Go ahead and get your degree. You can decide later what to do with it." I was not convinced. I said that if I accepted the call to be their full time pastor they would want me to be ordained. He said that it was only right that they should want me to perform weddings, preach funerals and baptize their children and that if I did those things I should be ordained. I was doing most of that already, except for the weddings, but I knew that if I accepted their call I would need to be ordained.

I wrote my father and told him what was happening. He was careful not to influence me any more than his unspoken influence was already working on me. I told him that if I accept the call I wanted him to preach the ordination sermon. He wrote back and said he would come for my ordination if he had to walk all the way from California.

When the committee came back the third time I accepted their call to be their pastor. Dr. Patterson moderated the ordination service and gave the charge to the candidate and dad preached the ordination sermon.

Dr. Patterson continued to be an influence after the ordination. I began to think about going to the seminary. I visited Golden Gate

Seminary when I was out in California visiting with mom and dad. I asked Dr. Patterson if he would recommend me. He said that he would be glad to recommend me if I insisted but that I should think seriously about. He said, "God needs good architects just as much as he needs good ministers."

In retrospect Dr. Patterson had incredible insight. He sent me to Dunwoody. He realized or sensed that I could do what that little church needed but he also knew that the ministry might not be my life's profession. That kind of thinking was radical in 1960. Most people did not think that way. The concept was that if you were called into the ministry you were called for life. Everyone, even non-church people encouraged me to stay in the ministry but Dr. Pat's wise counsel helped me know that just because God used me in a remarkable way at Dunwoody it did not necessarily follow that I should be a professional minister.

HOSPITALITY

"And a certain woman named Lydia ... besaught us, saying, if you have judged me to be faithful to the Lord, come to my house and abide there."
Acts 16:14&15

THE FIRST SUNDAY I TOOK MARY JO AND KAREN WITH ME TO Dunwoody Baptist Church, Mary Bob Kirby, met us after the service and said, "Preacher, you are coming home with us." She had five daughters. One of them said in a hushed tone, "Mama what are we going to feed them"? She said, "Don't worry, we'll find something after we get home."

The Kirby's lived in a small modest house that Steve Kirby had built with his own hands. They never apologized for their home. Their hospitality and warm affection wiped away any concern there might have been about the house. It was a primary example of the old saying, "A house is not a home."

The two oldest daughters, who were just a few years younger than Mary Jo took her in tow. The two youngest daughters, who were about the same age as our daughter Karen, took care of her and Mary Bob sat me at the kitchen table. It was actually a picnic table with benches tucked into a corner of the kitchen.

She gave me a big glass of ice tea (she always had a large jug of ice tea) and started talking. She was a talker! We talked about the Dunwoody community, about the church, about people who should be visited by the new preacher, (as if I was the new preacher) and talked about my sermon. I did not consider it a sermon but she wanted to talk about it.

Eventually she had fried two chickens, opened up two jars of home canned green beans, made mashed potatoes and gravy and baked a big tray of biscuits. She served us all in the grand tradition of fixing dinner for the preacher.

It reminded me of a story my father told:

"When I was a boy my father said, 'Johnny, go hitch up old Dan and take your mother down to Smith's Chapel. They've got a new preacher and she wants to hear him preach.' As we were going down the road, I thought, 'I sure hope she doesn't ask the preacher to come home with us.' She didn't bring home the preacher. She brought home two preachers."

"When we got home she said, 'After you get old Dan in his stall, go catch two chickens and chop their heads off. I'll put water on the stove to boil so you can pluck 'em.' While I caught the chickens, plucked them and cut them up to be fried, mother fixed the vegetables and the biscuits. My mother and the two preachers ate and talked all afternoon. I thought they would never leave. Late in the afternoon she said, 'Johnny, you had better take the preachers back to the Chapel, they've got to preach tonight.'"

Country families knew how to be hospitable.

The next Sunday, Connie Bishop (Mary Bob's sister in law) said, "Preacher you are coming home with us." It was months before Mary Jo had to prepare lunch after the Sunday morning service.

We ate with every family in the church. Dunwoody, in those days, was by and large a working class community. There were a few people with a college degree and a few with professional or management positions but the majority were mechanics, farmers, steel workers and other labor intensive professions. Some of the church members had a limited education and a few came to church in overalls and gingham dresses. They were all good people and when it was "Their turn" to feed the preacher, the house was clean and neat and the food was good. They put on their best "feed" and we appreciated it.

Hospitality was a vital part of the ministry. Hospitality goes both ways. You knew you were accepted when you went to someone's house for Sunday dinner and they knew they were accepted as valuable members of the congregation.

Times have changed since my father was a boy and times have changed since I was the young pastor of a little rural church. In those days there was not a "Cracker Barrel" in every small town and a fast food establishment on every corner.

Access to commercially prepared food does not mean we do not need to be hospitable We need to consider how to extend hospitality in the 21st centaury. How do we tell people they are welcome to our fellowship? How do we share the love of Jesus Christ with others?

ORDINATION

Dr. A. Scott Patterson, Rev. Buren Dowdy, who followed Dr. Pat as pastor of Clairmont Baptist Church, Rev. Brantly Seymore, pastor of the First Baptist church of Roswell, my father and several others were on the Ordaining Council. The service was at 3 pm on Sunday afternoon and the Ordaining Council met at 1 pm. I preached for the Sunday morning service. Dad said that I preached from the 53rd chapter of Isaiah. Dad preached the Ordination sermon.

When the council met they elected Dr. Patterson as the President. I had studied doctrine for weeks. I had no idea what kind of questions they might ask. I wrestled with atonement, justification, original sin, the unpardonable sin, mercy, salvation, the trinity and all kinds of doctrinal issues. I did not have a seminary education. I was not exactly comfortable. I could not imagine that they would not recommend me for ordination but I was not very cocky about it.

The ministers asked me several questions but I don't remember what they were. Dr. Pat waited until they had finished then he said, "Now Andy you just relax. I only want to ask you four questions."

"Why are you a Christian?"

"Why are you a Baptist Christian?"

"Why are you a Missionary Baptist Christian?"

"Why are you a Cooperative Missionary Baptist Christian?"

I said to myself, "Thank you Lord!"

SLEEPING DEACONS

I DIDN'T UNDERSTAND IT. THE DEACONS WERE SLEEPING DURING MY sermons!

After the church asked me to stay for a few months, I sought the advice of my mentor Dr. Scott Patterson. I needed to know how to prepare sermons. I also called my father, who was doing pioneer missions work in California. I had no training in sermon building. I was the teacher for a class of junior high school boys. The church gave me a teacher's guide. There was no guide for sermons. We Baptists did not even use the liturgical calendar.

I had filled in for Dr. Patterson a few times and he always suggested a topic and helped me with an outline and my father sent me some sermon outlines. I even remember one that he sent. It was about King David's kindness to Mephibosheth, the lame son of Jonathan.

It wasn't long, however, before I realized that Dr. Patterson and my father were limited resources. I also had the problem of being a full time architectural student. Design presentations and problems in integral calculus took most of my time.

I went to the book store and bought sermon outline books. I read sermons by Jonathan Edwards, W. A. Criswell, William Barclay and other famous preachers.

I took those sermons and outlines and modified them so that they related to the conditions at Dunwoody. I added my own stories and experiences and created what I thought were reasonably good sermons. My style was not good. I was still very nervous and unsure of myself but I thought my content was good.

I knew I was no Billy Graham, but it still bothered me that the deacons went to sleep. Steve Kirby never lasted more than five minuets and a few minuets later Mr. Swancy was gone. Alvin Price and Gordon Bishop nodded off some of the time. If it had not been for Mary Bob Kirby taking notes as fast as she could write and Mrs. Lucy Anderson's big smile I don't know what I would have done.

What I did, was go to see Dr. Patterson. I told him what was going on. I was about ready to give up the whole thing. He asked me how I was preparing my sermons and I told him. He thought about it for a few minuets and then said, "I think I know what your problem is." I was very relieved. I expected him to go to his library and get some books or give me some lessons in the art of preparing sermons. His response was, "You have been reading too many books. You are preaching way over their heads. You need to simplify your sermons. Make them so that a nine year old can understand you. Then maybe some of your deacons will understand."

He said, "Remember, if you say one sentence that two or three people remember for one day you have preached a tremendous sermon. Keep it simple. The whole Gospel is quite simple. God's love for man was demonstrated by the life, death and resurrection of Jesus Christ. That love is now active by the power of the Holy Spirit. When people confess their sins and accept Jesus as their Savior, they become part of the Kingdom of God and their lives will never be the same."

He added, "No matter what your sermons are about or where you take your text, you must always, somehow, tell your people that God loves them."

Then he paused and spoke very confidently, "And don't worry about your deacons going to sleep. They are hard working men and they need their rest. You will probably find that the ones who go to sleep first will be the ones who will give you the most support. Your job is to preach the Gospel and love your people. If your deacons need to sleep, let them sleep."

THE CAT

When we lived in Dunwoody our daughter, Karen, was 5 years old. She had a kitten but I don't remember its name, its color or anything about it. It was just a cat.

One day we realized it was missing. We looked everywhere but could find no sign of it. After it had been gone several days I told Karen that it probably had been killed by a stray dog and that I would get her another one.

Late one night after everyone else had gone to bed and it was very quite in the house I was in the study reading. I suddenly realized that I was hearing something. It was one of those situations where the sound is so faint that you don't even realize that you are hearing it. It was as if my sub-conscious was hearing it and I was slowly being tuned in to it. I finally realized that I was hearing the cat meowing. Once I knew that it was the cat I listened very carefully. The sound was coming from below the floor.

There was a partial basement under the house. I said, "That silly cat has been in the basement all this time." I thought maybe it had been hurt or was sick so I went down into the basement to find it. I called and sure enough it cried louder but it did not come to me. I decided to stand very still and be quite so I could determine where the sound was coming from.

The sound was coming from a hole in the foundation wall. The hole was about six feet above the floor and was about 18 inches wide and 16 inches high. It was in a wall that separated the main part of the basement from the area under the study. I had never been through that hole. I crawled through it into a crawl space that was about two feet high.

The sound of the kitten crying was louder but I could not see it anywhere. I shined my flashlight into every crook and cranny I could find but there was no cat. Finally I saw a rock wall. The floor joists were sitting on top of the wall. When I crawled over to the wall and looked over the top of it I was looking into an old well. It was probably

30 or 40 feet deep but it was dry. Walking around the bottom of the well was the cat.

I knew that I couldn't get through that hole. It was only 9 1/2 inches high and 15 inches wide. I went back into the house and got some rope, a can with a handle on it, some water and some food. I lowered the food and water into the well.

The next morning, I told Mary Jo about the cat. We thought, "If we could get the cat into a basket we could pull it up." We tried everything we could to get the cat into the basket. Once or twice the cat got in the basket, but when I tried to pull it up, it jumped out. I didn't know how I was going to get that cat out of the well.

I was frustrated. I could see the cat but I couldn't get it out of the well. I told Mary Jo that I didn't know how we were going to get it out. She said, "Call Steve Kirby. He can do anything."

Steve was one of the deacons in the church. He was a small man who had done hard physical labor all of his life. He was hard as a rock and had never met a problem he couldn't solve.

I called Steve. I was a little embarrassed. I told him that I didn't know what he could do that I had not already tried. He took one look at the situation and said, "I'll just go down there and get it." I said, "How are you going to do that? Are you going to cut a hole in the study floor?" He said, "No, I'll just go through that hole." I said, "You can't do that. That hole is too small for a man to get through." He said, "You just watch me."

He tied a rope around his waist and rolled up into a ball with his feet in the hole and his fanny up against the underside of the floor. His head was in the dirt. He started wiggling and squirming and eased himself backwards through the hole and into the well. He chimney climbed down the well. I kept the rope tight in case he slipped.

The cat was scared to death. It ran all over the bottom of the well trying to get away from him. Eventually he caught it and put it in the basket but every time I tried to pull it up the cat would jump out. After several attempts Steve simply caught the cat and held it to his chest and started climbing back up the wall of the well. The cat cried and clawed and scratched and hung on to Steve for dear life. When he got close to

the top he said, "Get this cat off of me!" I got the cat and put it down and it ran like a scalded dog. It was several days before it calmed down enough to let Karen touch it. It was skittish for as long as we had it.

Steve crawled out of the well with a great big grin on his face. He said, "First time I ever rescued a cat for the preacher."

THE FUNERAL

THE PAIN IN THE MIDDLE OF MY BACK WAS MADDENING. IT WAS RIGHT between my shoulder blades; up high. It was a sharp "catch" that seemed to cut me every time I breathed.

I had finished the Wednesday night prayer meeting service and conducted the choir practice and was finally back home in my study reading once again a chapter in the history of Baroque architecture when the telephone rang. I looked at the clock. It was after 11 PM. I wondered, what is wrong? Who is sick? Whose child has been hurt? A pastor always dreads the middle of the night telephone call.

A neighbor of Emmitt and Mary Dutton was on the telephone. I had never met the man. He said that his aunt who had lived in California had died and her body had been shipped back for burial. There was a little tone of desperation in his voice. He said that he had called the Methodist preacher and the Presbyterian preacher and the pastor at Sandy Springs and no one could conduct the service. He apologized for calling me but he said that Mary Dutton had said that her preacher would help him.

I really didn't want to do it. I didn't know the people. I would have to cut classes. I wondered what I could say about a lady I didn't know; to a family I didn't know. But the man seemed to be at his wits end and I didn't want to disappoint Mary Dutton and I guess I was young and something of a soft touch so I told him I would help him. I agreed to meet them at the Roswell Funeral Home the next morning at 10 o"clock. The grave side service would be at a cemetery a few miles north of Roswell. I fumbled through my book of funeral sermons but nothing seemed appropriate so I decided that I would simply read the 23 Psalm, a few verses from the 14th chapter of John and the assurance passage from the 15th chapter of I Corinthians, and say a few things about the love of God.

Baroque architecture is a boring subject after midnight so it wasn't long before I was asleep. I drug myself back to the bedroom and tried to find a position to ease the pain in my back and get some sleep.

When I woke up the next morning the pain in my back was worse. Mary Jo said, "Why don't you go to the doctor?" I hate going to the doctor, especially for something like a pain in my back. If I had broke a bone or cut myself I could justify going to the doctor but a pain in the back would go away eventually if I would just tough it out. I didn't want to waste the money.

I must have been hurting pretty bad because I gave in to go to the doctor. I said, "I can't think. I can't move. I can't do anything, with this pain in my back. I called Jean Kirby, one of the young ladies in the church who worked in a doctor's office and she said for me to come on over.

I drove to the doctor's office in Chamblee and Jean put me on some kind of sonic device. After a while the muscles in my back began to relax and I began to go over in my head the schedule for the day.

The first thing I thought of was the funeral. I looked at me watch and it was 9:45. Roswell is at least 20 miles from Chamblee. I came off the table half dressed and started running through the office. I told Jean that I had forgotten about the funeral. Why I didn't simply tell Jean to call Roswell Funeral Home and tell them to wait on me I don't know.

I jumped into the car. I was driving a 1957 TR-3 sports car and the top was down so I literally jumped into the car. I burned rubber through 3 gears and took off toward Roswell. The road was two lane and crooked. I down shifted into every curve and powered out of it. I kept a sharp look out for traffic out of side roads and for farmers on tractors but still I hit 100 miles an hour on some straight stretches of road.

When I got to the Roswell highway, US 19, I saw a county patrolman. I screeched to a halt beside him and told him my problem and asked him to escort me into town. He said that he couldn't do that but he would radio ahead and tell his buddies to let me through.

I left the car in the middle of the street in front of the funeral home and ran into the chapel. It was empty. One of the undertakers said that they had left for the cemetery about ten minutes ago. I thought, if they drive slow I might be able to catch them.

I jumped back into the car and started north to the cemetery. I calculated in my head that if they drove 35 miles and hour and I drove 90 miles and hour and if they would wait a few minutes for me I might make it.

No such luck! When I got to the cemetery there was no one there except two old men filling in a grave with a back hoe. They said, "You must have passed them. They left a few minutes ago."

I believe that the drive from the cemetery to Emmitt Dutton's neighbor's house was the longest drive I have ever experienced. I have been involved in some long distance driving. One trip to California I drove over a thousand miles in one day but that 15 mile drive from the cemetery was the longest of all.

I had to go. I couldn't pretend that it had not happened. The fact that there were extenuating circumstances didn't matter. I had forgotten a funeral!

I knew they would be disappointed, upset and perhaps even furious. On top of all that my back was really hurting. I drove into the yard. I sure didn't want to go up to the front door but I did. The door was opened by a man in a Army major's uniform. I said, "I'm the preacher and I forgot your aunt's funeral." He replied, "That's all right. Come on in."

Over the next few minutes there was one of those awkward scenes that would be funny if it was not about such a serious matter. I kept trying to explain why I had forgotten the funeral and he was apologizing for calling me in the middle of the night to conduct a funeral for a lady I didn't know and for a family who were not members of the church. We were both talking at the same time.

Eventually I realized that the was not upset. He said, "I've had a lot of trouble with my back and I know how a back pain can drive you almost to desperation. I asked what he did when I didn't show up. He said, "You know, I was an officer on the front lines in Korea and I had to bury a lot of soldiers over there and I had my New Testament in my breast pocket so I read from the 14th chapter of John and the 15th chapter of I Corinthians and said a prayer and we buried her." He paused for a moment and said, "I didn't know my aunt very well and this made the service a lot more meaningful than it would have been otherwise."

I told him that he had done exactly what I had planned to do. He said, "Preacher I sure am glad you came by to see us." I walked away and never saw those people again but I will never forget the day I forgot the funeral.

DUNWOODY ▓▓▓▓▓▓▓▓▓▓▓▓▓▓▓▓▓▓▓▓▓▓▓▓▓▓▓▓

DURING THE FALL OF 1958 AND THE FIRST PART OF 1959 I WAS working on my architectural thesis at Georgia Tech. My thesis was the research and design of a new church building for the First Baptist Church in Dunwoody, Georgia. The research for the project led me to realize that the city of Atlanta was going to expand into the Dunwoody community much faster than anyone expected. I read the Metropolitan Planning Commission's publication, "Now for Tomorrow." The Commission predicted that Dunwoody would be the fastest growing area in suburban Atlanta. They expected the population to grow to over 6,000 by 1980.

My classmates, working on their Master's Degree in City Planning, were another source of information. Their studio was adjacent to mine. They were working with the Metropolitan Planning Commission staff to update the 20 year forecast for Atlanta.

They had drawn a map showing the probable location of the I-285 circumferential freeway. There was a large circle around the intersection of Chamblee Dunwoody Road and Mt. Vernon Road. It indicated a possible location for a large shopping complex. That was exactly where the church was located. The map had concentric circles of expansion all the way to the Chattahoochee River. I was surprised to find that I-285 would come within 2 miles of Dunwoody.

When I told some of the members of the community what I had seen they simply did not believe me. They did not want to believe that the quite little community of Dunwoody was going to become part of the bustling metropolitan area of Atlanta. I knew that Dunwoody was soon going to emerge from its dormant stage. I had been to California and I had seen what happens around a major intersection on a circumferential freeway.

Another factor that influenced the development was that Dunwoody is at a higher elevation than the top of Stone Mountain. Since the beginning of the city, affluent Atlanta residents had been expanding to the north. "Aunt Pitty Pat's house in "Gone with the

Wind" was north on Peachtree Street. The new society houses built before the Civil War were out toward Peachtree Creek. Most cities in the Southern United States expanded with wealthy people taking the high ground and poor people taking the low ground. Before the days of air conditioning it was only good sense. Atlanta's expansion in the 60's, 70's and 80's would be no different. The Dunwoody farmer and blue collar workers would soon be overwhelmed by white collar professional families.

The spring and summer of 1960 brought the start of construction of two 125 house sub-divisions in Dunwoody. These houses were higher priced that any house in Dunwoody. "For Sale" signs were going up on many farms and tracts of land that had lain fallow for many years. It was obvious that the long expected in-flux of sub-division houses was on its way.

New families moving to Dunwoody spurred our efforts to enlist Baptist families into the First Baptist Church of Dunwoody. By the time the moving van had finished unloading, someone would call me and I would be on the doorstep telling them about the church in Dunwoody. I always got a warm reception. People would say, "We have always supported the local Baptist Church in our community. You can look for us next Sunday." Or they would say, "We would be glad to come and be a part of the small growing church you describe." Or, "Tell us exactly where you church is. We don't want our children to miss Sunday School more than necessary." But the next Sunday they were not to be found at First Baptist Dunwoody. A week or so later I go see them and they would say, "Tell us again about your church. Are you really Southern Baptist?" I would go over the details of our programs and tell them how much we needed them. After another week or so I would go back and they would say, "We're sorry but we have decided to go in to Wiecua Road or to First Baptist Chamblee or to Providence Baptist in Sandy Springs or some other church closer to Atlanta." I heard people say over and over again that their neighbors had told them that the Dunwoody Church was "Hardshell" or that they had heard that that little church has had a lot of trouble or some other remark that made them apprehensive about the church. They would say, "We drove by but we couldn't find a place to park." The church property was less than an acre and on Sunday morning cars would be parked up and down the road for quite a distance.

This theme was repeated over and over again. We talked to Baptist families in Dunwoody who went to other churches, we talked to our Methodist friends, we talked to out friends at the elementary school and anybody else who might have insight in our problem. It became obvious that there was a stigma associated with the First Baptist Church that was going to be very difficult to overcome.

The physical appearance of the little church was another problem. It was a converted World War II army barracks. The men of the congregation had renovated it with their own hands. It was adequate for a small semi-rural congregation but it was not modern in any way and neither did it have the charm of a historic country church. It was also on the wrong side of the road. It was north of Mt. Vernon Road. In the early 60's all of the new construction was on the south side of Mount Vernon Road. The property north of Mt. Vernon was still relatively rural. New residents of Dunwoody who lived south of Mt. Vernon were orientated toward Atlanta and seldom went to the north side of the community.

All of these factors; information from the research for my thesis, insight from the City Planning students, the frustration of trying to enlist new families, information gathered from community leaders and my knowledge of how Baptist churches were formed in growing communities led me to the conclusion that a new Baptist work would be started in Dunwoody very soon. I knew that if the First Baptist Church was not a part of that work it would be by-passed and would eventually die on the vine. When the residual Dunwoody families sold their property to developers and moved out to a more rural environment the church would die.

I went to see my mentor, Dr. Patterson. We discussed the situation many times. We wanted to find a way to save the years of effort that had gone into the little church and we wanted maintain the enthusiasm and high spirit that had developed in the church during the last two years.

At the same time we wanted to attract the new Baptist families who were moving into the community. We wondered if the Atlanta Baptist Association would help us. We knew that the Association was primarily interested in helping mission churches. We knew that in due time a mission would be started in Dunwoody. We wondered if the people in the Dunwoody church would consider the possibility of becoming a part of a mission. On the surface it seemed incredulous.

The Dunwoody church was 75 years old. They had a strong tradition. Many of the men had built the building with their own hands. There were strong emotional ties; for example Reverend Walter Anderson, Kenneth Anderson's father had been the pastor back in the 1940's. There were many reasons that made the idea that the Baptist of Dunwoody might be willing to give up the church they had been working 75 years to build seem ridiculous at best but Dr. Patterson was fond of saying, "Do not underestimate the power of God to work a miracle in the hearts of his people."

I began to talk to the leaders of the church. I had a private, confidential conversation with every deacon. Every one of them thought the idea a changing from a church to a mission was the strangest idea they had ever heard of. But, they also knew that something had to be done. Most of them said that if that was what had to be done they would do it. Others said, "Andy. I know that something has to happen but I don't know that my family can be a part of it, but we will not oppose it." Some of the people knew they would not be comfortable in a church with doctors, lawyers and business executives. At the conclusion of my round of discussions I was convinced that the church would do whatever was necessary to develop the kind of church the community needed.

I do not remember the circumstances that led me to Dr. J. T. Ford, pastor of the Wiecua Road Baptist Church. Wiecua Road was one of several churches that could have been interested in sponsoring a mission in Dunwoody but it seemed to me that Wiecua was the most logical one. They were missions minded, they were close to Dunwoody (but not too close) they were large enough to have the necessary resources and there were several members of Wiecua living in Dunwoody.

I remember driving to that big church and circling around the building several times to find the door and the courage to go in.

I told Dr. Ford's what I had in mind. I told him that I thought that the First Baptist Church of Dunwoody would be willing to become part of a mission if the mission was sponsored by a church like Wieuca Road. He said that what I was talking about was the craziest idea he had ever heard of but it might just work. He said that Wieuca Road had a strong missions committee and that Dr. Solomon F. Dowis, was the chairman. Dr. Dowis had retired from the Home Missions Board of the Southern Baptist Convention. We agreed that I would go back and start the process of getting the Dunwoody Baptist Church to ask the Wiecua Road Baptist Church for help and he would begin to talk to Dr. Dowis and other members of the committee.

The deacons of the First Baptist Church of Dunwoody presented a resolution to the members on September 3, 1960. The resolution detailed the conditions of the community and of the church and recommended that the church solicit advice, suggestions and aid from the Wiecua Road Baptist Church. The resolution was signed by Mr. Alvin Price, Chairman of the Deacons.

The Wiecua Road Baptist Church received the resolution and reported on October 14th that they had voted unanimously for their missions committee to proceed with negotiations to establish a working relationship. A committee of four people from Wiecua was elected to be on the committee and five members were from the church in Dunwoody. The committee was; Dr. Solomon F. Dowis, Chairman, Mr. Judson Garner, Mr. M. P. Snipes and Mr. O'Neil Hutcheson and from the Dunwoody church, Mr. Alvin R. Price, Mr. W. Kenneth Anderson, Mr. Clarence Autry, Mr. Paul Manning and Mr. Rodney Calvert. Dr. J. T. Ford and I were ex officio members. The bulletin from September 11, 1960 noted that Dr. Ford would be visiting the Dunwoody Church during the fellowship hour following the evening worship service.

A banquet was planned for April 21st, 1961. The invitation said:

The Wieuca Road Baptist Church
Requests the honor of Your Presence
At an
Introductory Banquet
To
Acquaint You with the Proposed
New Baptist Work in the
Dunwoody Community
Dunwoody Grammar School
Friday, April 21ˢᵗ, 7:30 p.m.

The letter on the inside of the invitation was from Dr. J. T. Ford.

Dear Friends:

What a thrilling prospect lies ahead of us. You of the community will have a new and growing Baptist work. We at Wieuca can encourage you, as others encouraged us seven years ago.

In order for you to know more about this opportunity, we want you and your family to be our guests at this banquet. A complete presentation of the proposed program will be given and adequate time allowed for questions. Your presence will not commit you in any way. This is a United Baptist endeavor. Full and unlimited cooperation has been received from the present Dunwoody Baptist Church, the Atlanta Baptist Association of Churches and our congregation.

I hope you can attend the banquet on Friday, April 21ˢᵗ. It will be a pleasure to meet you.

Sincerely Yours;
J. T. Ford

The church bulletin on May 7, 1961 contained a note from me to the congregation.

"My Dear Friends:

The time for mountain top rejoicing is now over. It is time to realize that the Lord has given us two months which to prepare for the great work that lies ahead. We cannot coast! The most careful, diligent and sustained effort that we can possibility put forth will be necessary to gird ourselves for the job ahead. We must never forget that God always expects the very best that you have. Do not expect a gravy train. You will have to <u>work</u> harder, <u>pray</u> more, <u>endure</u> more and <u>give</u> more than you ever have before. But the goal is worthy and God is on your side and through him you can have victory.

Love, Andrew"

Dr. Scott Patterson made one other significant contribution to my life. When it became apparent that a new effort was going to be organized in Dunwoody and that it was appropriate that I should step aside. I began to think about the future. I considered the possibility of preparing myself for full time professional ministry. I went to see Dr. Patterson for advice and his recommendation regarding Seminaries. He and I talked about the possibilities that were open for additional training and he graciously agreed to recommend me to any school I might want to attend. But he also said, "Son, don't think that just because God has used you in a very unique and wonderful way with the Dunwoody Church that is necessary for you to continue in the ministry for the rest of your life. God needs good architects just as much as he needs good ministers. Why don't you just wait and see what happens." Those brief comments jolted me out of the traditional thinking that I had about a "Call" to the ministry. Within weeks I had come to realize that my "Call" had been very specific. I had been called to help a church with a very specific problem. Now that the problem was being solved there was nothing that should keep me from going into the profession for which I had been trained.

The last few weeks before the organization of the new Baptist Chapel were spent helping the people get ready for the transition. I remember two sermons from that period of time. One was from II Kings 3:16 which reads:

"*Thus saith the Lord, make this valley full of ditches.*"

I used that ancient story about the people of Israel digging ditches in the desert, not knowing whether or not they would be filled with water, as an example of the faith the people of Dunwoody would have to have. I told them that it was their job to dig the ditches and wait for the Lord to fill them.

The other sermon was from Easter 4:14 which reads:

"*Who knoweth whether thou art come to the Kingdom for such a time as this*"?

The obvious application of that question to the situation at Dunwoody was that God had prepared the First Baptist Church of Dunwoody for 75 years to be the nucleus for a new Baptist work in the community. Even though it was made with a lot of pain, the members of Dunwoody Church had to know that the sacrifice they were going to make was worth the cost

In the first part of June 1961, I found a job with an architectural firm in Knoxville, Tennessee. On June 25th I preached the last sermon at the First Baptist Church of Dunwoody. After the sermon I called the church into conference and read the motion that disbanded the First Baptist Church. Letters were granted to those members who had indicated a preference to various surrounding churches and approximately 100 members were given letters to Wiecua Road Baptist Church to be part of Dunwoody Baptist Chapel. Open letters were given to those who had not made a decision, those who could not be found. The property was deeded to the Atlanta Baptist Association. We stood and wept and sang "To God be the Glory, Great Things He Hath Done" and walked out and closed the door. We met at 3 PM that afternoon at the Grammar School and became part of a new Baptist mission in Dunwoody. When that service was over I got in my car and drove to Knoxville to begin work as an architect the next morning.

In retrospect, it seems that God issued a specific. limitrd call for a unique ministry to a very special group of people in Dunwoody, Georgia. If I had not been a student at Georgia Tech and had special information and if I had not had a wise mentor in Dr. Patterson and if I had not been young and naïve enough but to believe that crazy and unheard of things could be done and if the people had not been wise enough to see the changes that were happening in their community and if they had not had the spiritual depth to be willing to sacrifice themselves, the Baptist work in Dunwoody would not have happened the way it did.

It was not essential that the First Baptist Church of Dunwoody give up its identity and become part of the Baptist Chapel. A new Baptist mission would have commenced in Dunwoody in due time regardless of what the First Baptist Church did. I think it can be said, however, that the action of the people in Dunwoody gave the work a tremendous boost which went a long way toward establishing the strong church that is in Dunwoody today. If events had not developed as they did, Wieuca Road Baptist Church would not have been the sponsor, the Atlanta Baptist Association would have not lent its credit and the property at the intersection of Mt. Vernon Road and Ashford Dunwoody Road would not have been available for the church.

The miracle was that the people dared to listen and respond to a plan of God that was unusual, daring and risky. The result was one of the strongest Baptist Churches in the South.

SECTION THREE

Section three is stories from my years when I was a member of Second Baptist Church in Memphis, Tennessee.

1. BROOKS RAMSEY
2. JAMES HATLEY
3. THE PRODIGAL SON
4. IT WORKS
5. HATLEY'S OFFICE
6. THE TRUTH
7. CHORES
8. LIFE AND DEATH
9. MUSIC IN THE RAFTERS
10. THE GRACE OF TALESTS
11. BE CAREFUL DAD
12. BRAZIL
13. THE GUN
14. COWBOYS AND INDIANS
15. INTO THE DEEP
16. FOUR REASONS
17. GREAT GREAT GRANDPAPPY
18. STUPID
19. YOU SURE DO LOOK GOOD
20. NOT YOUR PROBLEM
21. VERNON GREEN

BROOKS RAMSEY

The Adult Seven Sunday School Department at Second Baptist Church, Memphis, Tennessee, arranged for a two day retreat at the Pickwick Lake Lodge. They asked Dr. Brooks Ramsey to be the retreat leader. Brooks had been our pastor in the late sixties and early seventies. He selected the topic, "A New Way Home" and suggested the following readings: Isaiah 40-55, "chapters 1-3 from "Cadences of Home" and chapters 1-2 from "Finally comes the Poet" both by Walter Brueggemann.

The Department leader called several days before the retreat and asked if I would introduce Brooks. I thought about all of Brooks' degrees and all the churches he had served as pastor and all the other accolades that are normally cited in an introduction. On further consideration I knew that most of the people at the retreat would know those facts as well as I did. After some deliberation I decided to tell about my early experience with Brooks.

I moved to Memphis on April 2, 1968. You know what happened on April 4, 1968. The tragedy of Dr. Martin Luther King's assassination shook this city and all the rest of the country.

During the next few days the whole nation was consumed with talk about the events that happened in Memphis, Tennessee. My new co-workers and I were no exception. There were many conversations about race relations, the equality of all of God's people and the need for all races to support the civil rights movement. It was obvious that my convictions and beliefs were not as conservative and many people living in Memphis.

One of my new friends, who did not attend anybody's church said, "There is only one Baptist Church in this city that is right for you." I, of course, wanted to know where to find this church. He told me that it was "Way out on Walnut Grove Road" and that it is called "Second Baptist". He went on to say that they had a young preacher who some people consider a prophet.

I thought, "A Prophet!" "I'd better go hear this preacher." So I went to Walnut Grove and Perkins. The parking lot was full; cars were parked in the yard and all up and down Walnut Grove Road. Uniformed officers were telling people where to park. I parked on the street and walked at least a block to the church.

And what did I find? I found a Prophet! To my wonder and delight he preached with authority and clarity and all those other adjectives that describe a prophet. And in addition to that he preached with compassion, tenderness and love.

I called Mary Jo, who was back in Knoxville selling the house and finishing the school year, and told her that I had found a wonderful church.

Brooks Ramsey was not only a man who preached the gospel, he lived it. He walked with other pastors to the city hall to ask the mayor to use consideration in dealing with the sanitation workers who were on strike. Some of the more conservative members of the church were upset.

The first Sunday I took Mary Jo and our children to Second Baptist was the day of the "Great Debate". Several of the deacons had asked for a motion of no confidence in the pastor. After a long debate the members of the church voted to affirm the pastor and then they voted the entire board of deacons out of office!

Later, when it came time to elect new deacons, Brooks Ramsey came knocking on my door. He asked if I would serve as a deacon. I told him that I wasn't sure he wanted me. He asked, "Why?" I told him that first of all I had been ordained as a minister and I did not see any need to be re-ordained as a deacon. That did not seem to be a problem. I then said that they were planning a memorial march for Dr. Martin Luther King and that I intended to be in it. He replied, "So will I." I went on to tell him that there were three or four cherished Baptist doctrines that gave me problems. He said, "Brother we need you."

I was happy to serve with Brooks Ramsey. He was willing to include me in spite of my doubts, my controversial stand on race relations and my beliefs that were considered "Liberal" by many good Baptist.

I thought about that earlier this year when I read the concluding statement in the February 22, 2001 edition of the "Memphis Flyer".

The reporter asked Brooks, "How do you feel about those who ran you out of town in the sixties when you stood up for civil rights?" Brooks replied, "The poet Carl Sandburg was asked, 'What is your least favorite word in the English language?' Sandburg replied, "Exclusive".

I present to you a compassionate prophet who proclaims the love of God - Brooks Ramsey.

ANDREW
OCTOBER 27, 2001

JAMES HATLEY ████████████████████

I REMEMBER HOW EXCITED I WAS THE FIRST TIME I HEARD JAMES Hatley preach. He came to our church at West Hills in Knoxville to preach a revival in the fall of 1967. He was intelligent! He was articulate! He was honest about the Scripture! His remarks were well thought out, his presentation was straightforward and he was easy to understand! I thought, "This is the best preacher I have ever heard."

I had heard some who were considered to be good; Wayne Ward, C. Roy Angel, Duke McCall, Louie D. Newton and others but in my opinion Jim Hatley was the best.

I was relived. I didn't think Southern Baptists had a preacher like Jim Hatley. Others could preach, others could expound, others could write, and others could counsel, but Jim Hatley could do it all. And he could also set an example for loving others that could not be matched.

A few years later, after we had moved to Memphis and Brooks Ramsey resigned as pastor of Second Baptist Church, I went to the chairman of the pulpit supply committee. I said, "I know a man who can preach. He is an editor at the Sunday School Board in Nashville. I don't know if he would come to Memphis but he sure can preach." The chairman said, "I'll call him and find out." The rest is history.

He accepted the call to be the interim pastor. He did not intend to leave his position at the Sunday School Board.

After about six months a great majority of the church members wanted him to become the senior pastor. He resisted for a while but eventually accepted the call. He was our pastor for the next 17 years.

THE PRODIGAL SON

NOT LONG AFTER JIM HATLEY BECAME THE PASTOR OF SECOND Baptist Church we were exposed to his passion for The Prodigal Son. I distinctly remember thinking, the second time he started reading the fifteenth Chapter of Luke, "Doesn't he know that he preached on The Prodigal three or four months ago?" I didn't know how fertile and creative his mind was. He took his text on The Prodigal but the sermon was completely different! Every time he started reading the fifteenth chapter of Luke I said to myself, "He's doing it again" and every time he challenged me with a new truth.

Every time a visiting preacher took his text from the fifteenth chapter of Luke there would be a perceptible ripple of laughter flow through the audience. Well, it wasn't exactly laughter it was more of a "doesn't he know that Hatley is the absolute master of Prodigal Son sermons?" expression of concern.

Jim Hatley was a man with a big heart but it had little to do with the pump that pushed blood through his body. His heart was formed by a life of unique experiences, tempered by both joy and sorrow and above all activated, enhanced and empowered by the love of God.

I visualize Jim's heart as a very large sponge with the capacity to soak up large amounts of God's love and hold it until his heart was squeezed by someone who needed to be loved. Then there would be an outpouring of God/Hatley love. There is a line in the song, "Stouthearted Men" that says, "Give me some men who are stout hearted men, who will fight for the right they adore." Jim Hatley made me want to modify the line to read, "God give us men who are sponge hearted men, who will love as Christ taught us to love."

I do not know that it is true but I like to think that it was Jim Hatley's sponge heart that drew him to the story of The Prodigal Son. The story of the loving father who refused to give up hope. The father who welcomed his wayward son home with open arms.

When Jim died I wrote that he was the kind of man who would make a skeptic want to believe in the afterlife. Most of us are willing to accept on faith the statements in the Bible about the spiritual existence called Heaven. Some of us admit that we do not understand it - it doesn't comply with the laws of physics and the scientists among us can not explain it - after all Jesus said that it is spiritual and not physical. If we could only understand the mystery of the Spirit of God perhaps we could understand the meaning of the afterlife. But the afterlife is not about understanding. It is about hope. It is about faith. It is about love.

We do know this, we have experienced this; the love of God extends far into the mysteries of life and it extends far into the mysteries of death. The love of Jesus Christ, sacrificing himself for mankind and the love of Jim Hatley living his life in service to others does not end in desth.

The visions, of the Apostle John, of pearly gates and golden streets may or may not be an expression of middle eastern mysticism but we can rest assured that his vision of the continuing power of God in this life and in the life to come is real. We may not know the mysteries of the afterlife but we do know that the love of God that empowers our lives today will continue to sustain us in the afterlife no matter what the exact manifestation might be.

The love of God as Jesus told it in the story of The Prodigal Son and the love of God as it was demonstrated in the life of Jim Hatley is not something that will die. The mysteries of the afterlife are not frightening when they are surrounded by, enmeshed in and empowered by the love of God.

> "Stouthearted Men" from the musical "The New Moon." Book and lyrics by Frank Mandel and Oscar Hammerstein II, Music by Sigmund Romberg.

> PS:
> Several years after Jim Hatley died members of the church collected sixteen sermons on The Prodigal Son and published them. The title of the book is, "You Can Go Home Again" .

HATLEY'S OFFICE

Not long after Jim Hatley accepted the call to be the pastor of Second Baptist Church he asked me to help him redesign his office. Jim had served as interim pastor for several months and during that period of time he had worked out of the office that the previous pastor, Rev. Brooks Ramsey, had used. Now that he was the full time pastor, he wanted an office that was more compatible to his style of ministry.

He wanted a room that was designed more as a counseling room than an office. He felt that a room with walls full of books intimidated people. He didn't want to impress people with all the books he had read and he didn't want the books to be a source of distraction. He, on the other hand, did not want to have a separate room just for counseling.

He asked me if I could come up with a scheme that would provide three different areas in one room. He wanted a work area where he could write his sermons and he wanted his working library close by so that he didn't have to leave the room every time he wanted to look at a book and he wanted a counseling area that would be more like a living room.

We came up with a plan that took over one of the Sunday School rooms. We solved the problem of hiding the books by putting them behind a wing wall and we separated the work area from the counseling area by putting it on a raised platform at the back of the room. The front of the room would be furnished with living room furniture. He also liked the idea that children could sit on the steps to the raised platform. It was an unusual arrangement but it met his specific needs.

There was another reason for all of this activity. The church had recently hired a new minister of education and administration. Jim wanted the new minister to have the former pastor's office because it was adjacent to the clerical staff. He wanted every one to know that Tommy Bridges was in charge of administration. He wanted to distance himself from the daily administration of the church. Otherwise Tommy would never have full control and would always be second guessed.

Dr. Hatley brought the subject up at the deacons meeting. There was a long discussion about the cost of the renovation. The church was in dire straits from a financial standpoint and it was touch and go every month to make the cash flow work. Most of the deacons wanted their new pastor to have the kind of office he felt he needed but they didn't want to put any more strain on the church budget than absolutely necessary.

Several men spoke up and said that if we could get someone to donate the materials they would do the work. That way we could get the new office without it costing very much. Even so every deacon was not in favor of the project. They more or less took the position that if the old office was good enough for the former pastor, it was good enough for the new pastor.

One of the men who was most opposed to the office was Mr. C.B. Ramsey. C.B. was one of the most respected men in the church. He had been a deacon and a Sunday School teacher for many years. He had been the Chairman of the deacons during a year of great difficulty and stress and his great love for the church was well known and appreciated. C.B. was a very soft spoken man but he could be very intense. He was a sensitive, caring, gentle, humble man; he was not argumentative or confrontational but in this case he had strong feelings and he could not sit back and not express his opinion.

He walked very slowly to the front of the room. He was torn between his genuine desire to support his pastor and his feelings about what should be done about the proposed office. It was difficult for him to oppose his pastor and speak against what was clearly a majority opinion. None of that kept him from speaking his mind. He was almost in tears. I was reminded of the prophet Hosea who wept as he preached to the children of Israel.

His point of view was well reasoned and thought out. He had been a teacher most of his life and knew how to write and express his thoughts. He said that the office we already had was good enough for any preacher; we didn't have a dime of extra money to spend; the ladies needed their classroom. He capped off his appeal by saying that as far as he was concerned, Tommy Bridges could set himself up a little desk in the hallway somewhere.

He spoke passionately and eloquently against the motion and when the vote was taken, he voted against it. He was in a distinct minority. I thought that it was good that C.B. was able to speak his mind in the deacons meeting.

The motion was brought to the church at the next business meeting. I didn't think there would be any opposition to the motion. When the moderator asked it anyone wanted to speak against the motion I was surprised to see C.B. get up and slowly make his way to the front of the room.

I said to myself, "Oh no," he knows there is no chance the church will reject the motion. Why is he going to speak against it when he knows that he is going to loose?" The church was so glad to have Dr. Hatley as pastor they would have probably hung gilded paper in the office if he had asked for it. His speech to the church was no less passionate or eloquent than his speech to the deacons and the result was even more overwhelming against him.

The next Saturday a group of us met at the church to start the work on the new office. About ten o'clock I looked up and there came Mr. C.B. Ramsey with an old fashioned carpenter's tool box in his hand. I said, "C.B. I thought you were against this project." He said. "I was and I still am. I think it is unnecessary and a waste of money but, if my pastor wants it and if my church votes to do it, I will do whatever I can to help get it done."

He worked as long and as hard and anybody. It was one of the finest examples of a man's love for his church that I had ever seen.

IT WORKS

The news came that Dr. Hatley is in the hospital; in the intensive cardiac care unit.

He has been in poor health for several years. He has had two open heart operations and is now suffering with emphysema and I don't know what else. He has, because of the recent advances in medicine, already outlived his genetic code. If the heart by-pass operation had not been perfected he would have been gone some time ago.

That does not make the news any easier to bear. His influence on our lives and the lives of our children has been immense. He has been more than a pastor to me. He has been both friend and confident. We have had many "all guards down" conversations in which it was impossible to say whether he was counseling me, or I was counseling him. Very few people have had as close a relationship as Jim Hatley and I.

It is interesting that the relationship was not social. He and June have been to our house on special occasions and we went to their house a few times. He and I would go somewhere to get some veggies or some home style cooking.

Our relationship was a matter of infrequent but very close conversations. I would be walking down the hall outside his office and he would see me and say, "Come in and close the door." He would say, "What do you think about.." world events, the state of the nation, coming action by the government, (He knew about bussing long before anyone had any idea it was going to happen in Memphis). We talked about the city, the denomination, the church, his family, my family, his hopes and fears and dreams or my hopes and fears and dreams. It could be about almost anything but it was always without veneer or pretense. Sometimes it was my agenda and sometimes it was his.

Many of our conversations were about our children. We both had children who were a great source of pride and we had children who were a great source of concern. We both had a child who could not make it in the standard High School environment. Karen and Cavan both attended what was called "Occupational Emphasis Program". As they struggled through those difficult years Jim and I struggled together. Unfortunately, Cavan did not respond to the pressure of growing up as well as Karen.

We wept together when Cavan went to prison. We rejoiced together when it seemed that he was making a much needed adjustment and we grieved together when he got sick. In the early days of HIV dirty needles infected many young men.

Karen was also stricken with an illness that we both thought would take her away. When she was at the point of death we prayed and we shook with fear. Many times during that long nightmare I would be sitting in her hospital room and look up and see him standing outside the door. When he realized that I had seen him, he would come in and say all the right things to her but on his way out he would be shaking. I would go out into the hall and we would hold each other. He didn't have to talk and I didn't have to ask questions. The feelings that passed between us were more profound than words.

When, by the grace of God, Karen recovered, we rejoiced with more awe than celebration. When healing was assured, the wonder of knowing that miracles really do happen, bound us together closer than brothers.

I never had a friend who listened to me like Jim Hatley. Almost every person you talk with is thinking, all the time you are talking, about what they are going to say when you finish. Jim didn't do that. He listened to me and I tried very hard to listen to him. He is one of the few people I have ever known who really knew what Reuel Howe was talking about in his book, "The Miracle of Dialogue".

Now he is desperately sick. What can I do but pray?

I can rejoice that God chose a man like Jim Hatley to show the love of God to mankind.

I can rejoice that I was blessed to be his friend.

I can rejoice that I could share with Jim Hatley the joy that occurs when a miracle happens.

I can rejoice that I could share with him in the sorrow that occurs when the miracle does not happen.

I can rejoice that through the life of Jim Hatley, the "Good News" has been demonstrated. As Jim said many times, "When all is said and done, it really does work."

"The Miracle of Dialogue." Reuel Howe, The Seabury Press, New York.

THE TRUTH ▓▓▓▓▓▓▓▓▓▓▓▓▓▓▓▓▓▓

I was flying from Memphis to Raleigh and had to change planes in Cincinnati. A very well dressed elderly gentleman carrying a large bundle wrapped in terry cloth towels was assigned to the seat next to me.

He was having some trouble getting the package into the overhead compartment so I got up to help him. The package was not very heavy but it was rather bulky. I didn't pay much attention to what it was; people carry all sorts of packages onto the airplane these days. He was very concerned about the package. He asked me to be very careful with it.

He introduced himself as Mr. Smith and I was happy to tell him that I was Andrew Smith. It was not the first time I met a stranger named Smith.

After we took off, he asked me about my profession and I asked what he did for a living. He said that he was on his way to Richmond to give a lecture about Biblical manuscripts. He said that he didn't give as many lectures as he used to and that was OK because it gave him more time to do research in Europe. I asked him whether his research involved searching for old manuscripts or was he working in textural criticism.

He realized that I knew something about his specialty so we began a very interesting conversation. He told me that he owned one of the largest private collections of old bibles and old manuscripts in the United States. He said that he had a Tyndale and an early copy of the Gutenberg and a Breeches Bible and many other early printed bibles.

He took a little bundle of red velvet cloth out of the inside pocket of his jacket. He unrolled it very carefully and took out 4 small stones that had cruciform writing on all sides. The largest was about one inch square and 3/8 inch thick. He said that the stones were older than Abraham. He explained that the common documents like tax records or deeds or private letters would be carved into clay tablets but that very important documents would be carved into stone.

I asked him if he could read the inscription. He said that he had never learned to read cruciform writing. He was content to leave that up to scholars who were specialist in early Mesopotamian languages. The inscriptions had been deciphered and that he knew what they said.

The large bundle I helped him put in the overhead compartment was a Torah scroll. It was a large roll about 20 inches long with two sticks protruding out of its middle. He said that it was almost a thousand years old. I then realized why he was so nervous when I helped him put it away.

Mr. Smith said that he lives in Orlando, Florida and goes all over the United States and Europe to make presentations in churches about manuscripts and old bibles.

We talked about the great codices; Vaticanus, Sinaiticus and Alexandrius. He said that he rejected both the Vaticanus and the Sinaiticus because they had too many errors. We talked about the 5,000 or more manuscripts that are available to scholars to study. I asked him if it was true that there is no substantial conflict about basic doctrines in the manuscripts. He said that some people hold that opinion but that he felt obliged to reject writings that did not use the word "Virgin" when talking about the mother of Jesus. I didn't want to get into a debate with Mr. Smith so I did not press my views about Textural Criticism or biblical doctrine. It was obvious he was far more conservative than I am.

He talked about the fact that many of the English translations of the Bible are based on the work of Westcott and Hort and that they based their work on the Vaticanus and the Sinaiticus. He was genuinely concerned that many bibles are based on what he believed to be corrupt manuscripts. I asked him if the people who put together the new translations available today, the NIV, the NRSV, the NEB etc. did not take into consideration all of the available texts. He said that he believed that they all were based on the old Wescott and Hort translations and were therefore not correct.

He had apparently spent his life in a search of the authorative text. He was concerned that some translations are not strong enough on what he considered the primary doctrines; the virgin birth, the blood atonement and the reality of hell.

He asked me what I believed about those doctrines. I told him I had serious questions about all of them. He then asked me what "persuasion" I was. When I told him that I was Baptist he was flabbergasted.

He said that it was hard to believe that he and I could belong to the same denomination. I told him that I considered the diversity of beliefs and the freedom of private interpretation of scripture to be the strongest aspect of the Baptist faith. He asked me if I was a "Liberal". It was almost as if he had never seen one before. I told him that, if I understood the wide continuum of belief within Christianity, I was far from being a liberal. I said that I did not like labels but if I had to choose one, I would probably be somewhere between a neo-orthodox and a post-neo-liberal. In some ways I consider myself to be very conservative and on the other hand I am sure that there are many people who would consider me a wild eyed liberal.

I went on to say that I believed the people of God should be exposed to all interpretations of scripture. He asked if I thought an ordained catholic priest should teach Catholicism in a Baptist seminary. I said that I didn't see why he shouldn't because, as far as I was concerned, all truth is God's truth. Every person is responsible for conducting his own search for that truth. I believe if a person does not look at what other people believe he makes his choices in ignorance.

Mr. Smith said that he would have to agree that all truth is God's truth but he wanted a person well grounded in the fundamentals to do the teaching. He said that he would probably have to consider himself a fundamentalist.

I told him that I wasn't all that concerned about Catholics or Mormons or Buddhists teaching in our Baptist seminaries but that I was deeply concerned that the wide range of beliefs held by Baptist are not being taught. He agreed that I perhaps had a point.

It was very interesting to me to talk with Mr. Smith; a man who has spent his entire life in a search for the truth. He had defined the truth to be the words found in the authentic manuscripts of scripture. He probably would not be totally satisfied unless he was convinced that he had an autograph in his hands. I have no doubt that his search has been both genuine and devout. He has informed many people about the manuscripts and thereby enhanced their understanding of how and where the scriptures originated. His contribution should in no way be discounted. I told Mr. Smith I had absolutely no problem with his approach to the search for truth but I was concerned that there appears to be people in our denomination who want to deny me the right to disagree and still be considered a loyal Baptist.

I was amazing to me that a person so close to scripture, i.e.: the text could hold such a narrow interpretation. It must be remembered, however, that many of the best textural scholars down through the ages have come from the most conservative branches of the church.

The least that can be said is that the flight from Cincinnati to Richmond with Mr. Smith was one of the most interesting airplane flights I have ever taken.

CHORES

It had been 42 years since I left hone, but my father was just the same as he had always been when it came to chores. He always had a longer list than I could get done. I am sure that when I was born he said, "Great, as soon as we get this boy off the bottle I've got some things I want him to help me do."

Every time went for a visit, I knew he would have a list of things that needed to be done. I knew that I would have to clean up around the garden, but I soon realized he had things for me to do that I had not anticipated.

Before I started to work I went to the hardware store and bought a pair of work gloves and a handle for the axe. He was pleased about the axe handle until he found out that it cost almost 10 dollars. He said I should have been able to buy a whole new axe for 10 dollars.

I chopped up two old stumps that were at the edge of the garden and then cut down a small tree. I was worried that he would stumble over the stumps and break another bone. The tree was shading his garden.

He had allowed the area around the garden to grow up with weeds and blackberry vines and honey suckle vines until it looked like it was in a jungle. The ragweed was over head high and I knew when it bloomed it would trigger his hay fever. I got the riding mower started and began to run it into the high weeds. Most of the time I would have to back up and take two or three runs at the weeds before I could knock them down. It took quite a few runs around the garden to get most of the weeds mowed down. I was not able to do a lot of work around the old grape arbor. I decided that I would have to come back later in the summer and clean around the grape arbor.

I told him to sit in his recliner and watch the Braves but every time I looked up there he was hobbling down through the yard on his walker.

I told him it was too hot for him and insisted that he go back to the house. On his way back he stopped by the tool shed. The first thing I knew he had the shears and was snipping the bushes around the back porch. When I went to the house for a drink of water, he asked if I could find some way to cut the new growth out of the top of the holly bush. Three times I stopped the tractor and coaxed him back to the house. I told mother it was her job to keep him in the house but she said, "He never has done what I tell him to do."

After I got the yard work done and took the tractor back to the shed, dad had made his way back and asked if I thought I could get the blade off the mower and sharpen it. I was almost exhausted so I was not disappointed that I couldn't find a wrench big enough to get the lock nut off. By that time I was thinking that it sure would be good to get to the house, take off my shoes and get a glass of ice tea.

About the time I sat down he said, "If we could get that electric weed eater running we could clean up some of these old spring flowers around the porch." I got the weed eater out of the shed and let him stumble around the porch and whack a few weeds and flowers. He was exhausted in about 5 minutes so he sat on the porch and supervised while I finished the job. He told me exactly what to cut. "Get that one over there. Go ahead and trim around the garbage can and while you are at it might as well trim around the rose bushes."

When I finally got all the tools put up and cooled off enough to come in the house mother took up the task of "chores for Andrew." She said, "I sure wish you could fix that old towel rack in the bathroom." Old is one of her favorite adjectives. The way she uses "old" doesn't have anything to do with age. It has to do with the fact that she doesn't like it or that it won't do what she wants it to do. Even if she has a new pair of shoes that hurt her feet she will say, "These old shoes are awful. They never have been right." She uses the same system for people. If she doesn't like someone she will say, "Old so and so is in trouble again. I knew that he would never amount to anything" or "I just know that that old boy is up to no good."

Dad has from the time I can remember had a long list of things that needed to be done. When I was a teenager I used to accuse him of lying awake at night thinking of chores for me to do. No matter how quickly I did my chores there was always another one waiting for me.

I wanted a fixed list of things to do, so when I got them done, I could do what I wanted to do. No way! The list was endless.

I suppose that the list is and has always been endless. There are always more thing to do than can possibly be done. There are more repairs to do on the house, more stories to write, more work at the office, more sick people to visit more of every part of life to do than can possibly be done.

In a way that is a real blessing. To be needed is one of the things that makes life worthwhile. It is only when we are not needed, not wanted, not challenged that we are finished. I suppose it is good that one of the goals of life is to never get finished. Perhaps it is a blessing that at the end we simply run out of time.

LIFE AND DEATH

IT'S STRANGE — WE ARE ON VACATION IN A FAR AWAY COUNTRY - EXOTIC, at least to us - and my thoughts are on life and death.

I have a dear friend with a situation I cannot get out of my mind.

His mother, who was 96 years old, died.

His son, who was only 40 years old, committed suicide.

His daughter got married.

All within a three week period.

He knew his mother was going to die. We had shared concerns about our aging parents. I'm sure he had no regret in letting her go - except for the sorrow of losing physical contact with someone he loved. Even though he will miss his mother, I am sure he prayed every day for her release from the shackles of a frail old body.

But 40 and suicide - that hurts! That leaves a person numb - beaten - devastated. There are probably no more profound "Why" questions than the questions that come from the self termination of life at its prime. There is never a greater need for answers. No matter what is said, there are no answers.

Of course if we did not ask questions we would not be human - there would be no human progress if we did not ask questions. We would be like robots - but even "Data" on Star Trek has a circuit go bad occasionally and in his search for personhood he is always asking questions.

We simply can not gloss over tragedy with simple statements about the "Will of God" even though we know that the will of God encompasses all things. We simply can not be predestinarian about the will of God to the extent that we do not ask questions. We can not allow ourselves to think that tragedy is the direct will of God. The will of God! We - yes we are the ones who do it - make it such a harsh - uncompromising - uncompassionate - unloving concept. Have you ever noticed that "The will of God" is most often considered in the face of tragedy? When good things happen we are prone to take credit for them or ascribe them to fate. But tragedy - tragedy is panned off as the

"Will of God". It is simply not right. No matter how many proof texts we can find, the God of love can not be a God of tragedy!

Scripture is too full of God's yearning for good - too much striving for righteousness - too much longing for man to be holy - too much love in both the Old and New Testaments for us to pigeon hole God into a God who wills tragedy!

We all have a sickness unto death. I believe it was Jean Paul Sartre who said, "All grief comes down to one thing - we run out of time."

My friend said, "He had so much to live for" but he didn't. His son took his own life.

One of my partners had a heart attack. His wife said, "He died too young - He was only 61." But her husband's heart said it was time to stop.

One of my young friends said, "He left us too early". But her husband's heart stopped at 54 just the same.

It is a luxury, in a sense, to die on time - at the right time - with all preparations made - all good-byes said - peace with God assured. My father died that way. He sang the "Doxology", added the amen and faded away. The old body fought for two more weeks but he did not say another word. His time had come. It was the right time for him to go.

Few of us live in luxury and fewer still die a luxurious death.

We must remember that the human body is flawed. In one way or another there is a fatal flaw. The flaw can show up before birth and we call it a miscarriage. It can show up in early childhood and we call it Leukemia. It can show up in young adulthood and we call it MS. It can show up at almost any age and we call it cancer. With many mature men and women it is called heart attack, and later on we call it Parkinson's or Alzheimer's. If we survive all of that, we call it "Old Age" but in one way or another we are all flawed.

Sometimes the flaw is a matter of judgment like a teen age boy trying to out race a train and sometimes the flaw is emotional or mental and the result is what we call suicide. We must remember that one flaw is not more right or wrong than any other flaw. All flaws end in death. That is the way God made us.

The physical flaw given to Adam in the ancient stories in Genesis is the flaw we deal with today. The spiritual flaw of Adam, as Paul talked about it in Romans, was corrected by the sacrifice of Jesus but the physical flaw is still with us.

The love of God encompasses all our faults and the great diversity of our flaws. Regardless of the pain our flaws impose upon us, we must dwell on the magnificence of the love of God.

To use anthropomorphic language, we must remember that the arms of our loving God are long enough and secure enough and strong enough to encompass us, with all our faults, with all our flaws, with all our unanswered questions, with all our doubts, yes with all our humanity! Thank God!

MUSIC IN THE RAFTERS

"Verily, I say unto you, Inasmuch as ye have done it
unto one of the least of these my brethren, ye have done
it unto me."
Matthew 25:40

KEN BYRD WAS THE MINISTER OF MUSIC AT SECOND BAPTIST MEMPHIS. He had a wonderful tenor voice. If you go into the sanctuary and sit down and be very quite and listen very carefully you can hear, echoing up in the rafters, a lyric tenor voice. It is the voice of Ken Byrd. Some will hear "The Holy City" and others will hear "Why Should He Love Me So?" and still others will hear the "Sanctus" by Charles Gounod.

What I hear is a little different. One Sunday evening, in the late seventies, Ken gave a concert. He sang the "Sanctus" and his favorite hymns and some of the wonderful old gospel songs but he ended the concert with a series of Irish ballads. He sang "When Irish Eyes are Smiling" and "Mother McCrae" and finished with "Danny Boy". When he sang the lament of that heart broken father for his "Danny Boy", killed on the fields of Flanders, I thought my heart would break.

We used to argue, when we were in high school, about whether or not sound ever dies. The argument was that it gets fainter and fainter and fainter but it never dies. I don't know whether or not that is true but I do know that I can still hear the voice of Ken Byrd bouncing around in the rafters.

About ten years later Ken died. It was totally unexpected. The Sunday after the funeral his wife Peggy was sitting in her customary place in the balcony and I was sitting in my customary place a couple of pews behind her. I saw her sitting there and I knew that if I could hear Ken's voice bouncing around in the rafters it must have been the greatest musical crescendo in the history of the world in her head. So I reached down and picked up the bulletin and wrote her a short note. I didn't think much about it. I just wrote a spontaneous little note and gave it to her. The note said:

Jesus, do not take away the hurt,
Especially, when the hurt is all that we have left.
Let the hurt and all that it means to us
sanctify our lives so that we can
live in honor of that which we lost
and in anticipation of the tasks that remain
for us to accomplish in Your name.

I forgot all about that note.

Last year one of my writings was used on the front of the "Order of Service." The next Sunday I was sitting in my customary place and Peggy was in her customary place. She turned around and said, "You wrote something for me one time." I said, "I did?" She said, "I've still got it here in my billfold." Ten years later it was still in her billfold. She said, "I still take it out and read it now and then."

The point is; I wasn't thinking of doing a good deed for Jesus. I wasn't thinking of giving a cup of cold water in the name of Jesus. I simply saw my my friend, sitting there, hurting. I wrote her a little note. I've been writing notes to girls since I was five years old and in the first grade.

You never know when a spontaneous act of kindness will result in a meaningful and lasting benefit.

THE GRACE OF TALENTS

THERE IS A USED BOOK STORE ON THE DELTA AIRLINES CONCOURSE AT the Raleigh International Airport. I am a sucker for a used book store. I can not resist going in to see if a book will jump off the shelf at me. Most of the time I don't buy anything but this time I noticed the title, "In Africa with Schweitzer" by Dr. Edgar Berman.

I had never heard of Dr. Berman but I had certainly heard of Dr. Albert Schweitzer. One of the promotional quotes on the back of the book was, "Dr. Berman's talks with Albert Schweitzer provide fresh insight into one of the most remarkable men of our time." I was hooked. I forked over my five dollars and put the book into my briefcase.

I had read Schweitzer's "Quest for the Historical Jesus" and his "Memoirs from My Childhood and Youth" but I have not been a serious student of Schweitzer. I had a long layover and I read most of the book before I got home.

One of the things that Dr. Berman wanted to ask Dr. Schweitzer was why he decided to go to Africa to take medical care to the people of the rain forest. Schweitzer said that the primary reason he decided to go to medical school at 40 years of age and prepare himself for a life in the jungle was -

> "... to repay the grace of talents that had been visited
> upon me. The best way was by relieving at least some
> of the physical misery of our world. Also, spiritually,
> I felt a deep responsibility to all men. I decided that
> would make my life my argument - going to Africa
> was living it""

I have often wondered why one of the most brilliant men of the 20th century would gave the biggest part of his life to serve primitive people in the rain forest of Africa. He was one of the most respected organists of his day. His interpretations of Bach are still the benchmark for the study of Bach's music. He was the most famous organ builder and restorer of historic organs who has ever lived. He was a first rank philosopher and his early writings, especially his "Quest for the Historical Jesus" established him as one of the most visionary theologians of the century. To most rational men, Schweitzer's going to Africa was a colossal waste of talent.

Just imagine how much he could have done in any one of his fields of endeavor if he had stayed in Europe. Or, he could have immigrated to the United States like Albert Einstein and exerted enormous influence on both music and theology. He went to Africa to express his gratitude for the great gifts bestowed upon him.

The gift of the Love of God that is bestowed on each of us is just as valuable as the gift bestowed on Dr. Schweitzer. We may not have great musical or philosophical or theological or medical gifts like Schweitzer but our gift of grace is just as important as Schweitzer's gift of grace.

What do we give? How do we express our gratitude? How do we serve our fellow man? What are the words of the old hymn?

> "I Love Thee, I Love Thee,
> I Love Thee my Lord, …
> But how much I love thee,
> My actions will show."

Anonymous 1805

BE CAREFUL DAD

What a strange reversal of roles,
He is 83 and I am 57
And I am giving him a driving lesson.

Dad, the last time I rode with you, you scared me.
You turned the steering wheel with short little movements,
And you made wide sweeping turns,
Like a semi-trailer truck.

"This new medicine is doing a lot of good.
I think I can drive just fine now.
Lets' go for a spin and I'll show you."

"Lets' go for a spin and I'll show you."
I think I used those exact words when I was 14.
Pestering him to let me drive the old chevy.

It's strange -
I'm sitting here on the passenger side,
Watching him like a hawk -
And he is nervous about his driving test.

"I am glad you came to see me, son.
It sure has been boring, not able to go anywhere, -
And I don't like having to depend on other people,
even if they are kin."

"I don't want to be beholden to anybody."

Now dad I want you to avoid that bad intersection at the foot of the hill.

"Okay - your sister, your mother and your cousins
have all been fussing about that intersection.
I guess I'll have to go the long way around."

Be sure to look in both directions
when you get to the crossroads.
In fact dad, look both directions twice.
Your reaction time is slow.
A car can be on top of you before you know it.

"Son, we've got to get out of here sometime.
If I wait until it is completely clear
we may have to sit here all afternoon.
See, we zoomed across that road with no trouble at all."

"I've been driving for 63 years without an accident of any kind and
now everybody is worried that I'm going to kill myself."

Yes dad - but it is the first accident that we are
worried about.

Dad - you are doing much better.

Dad, don't follow too close.
It takes you longer to get your foot on the break than it used to.

Dad, don't go too fast.
If people honk their horn at you, just let them honk.

"It's like going back to when I learned to drive the old "T" model Ford.
I have to pay strict attention to my driving.
I look at the road ahead and decide what I am going to do a long
time before I get there."

Dad, do you see that little car behind that truck up there in front of us?

"Yes son, I see it ."

What color is it?

"Blue, I think."

Good, but remember that you still have one bad eye.

Don't get caught out after dark.

Well dad, you passed your driving test.

But don't forget, I'm going to be checking on you.
The neighbors all watch for me.

Dad - you know that someday you'll have to give it up.
Someday it simply will not be safe anymore.

    "Yes son -
    But I'm not going to do it until I have to."

Be careful, dad.

BRAZIL

June the 21ˢᵗ 1978 was our 25ᵗʰ wedding anniversary. More than a year in advance I started planning and saving money so I could surprise Mary Jo with a "25ᵗʰ Anniversary Cruise". I had talked to several travel agencies and set a tentative date.

Sometime in the spring our pastor, Dr. Jim Haley, started talking about taking a group of young people on a mission tour to South America. He believed that the best way to inspire young people with the need for missions was let them experience it first hand.

Jim has been involved, for many years, with a group called South American Missions. One of his classmates in collage, Eduardo Lasa was from Brazil. When he finished his studies he went back to Brazil and founded a church and a school in the city of Parintins. Parintins is on island in the Amazon River a few hundred miles down stream from Manaus. It is located right in the middle of the Amazon River basin. The only way to get to the city is by boat or air.

Jim arranged a trip that left the States at Miami and flew to Manaus, Brazil. They went down the Amazon River on a boat to Parintins. After a week or so in Parintins they went to Brasilia, Rio, Salvador, Beliean and then back to Miami.

Mary Jo did not know about the money I had stashed away for the cruise. I didn't know what to do when she started talking about how much she wished our son Steve could go on the mission trip.

When she gets something like that on her mind she can be very persistent. I thought about it for a long time. I really wanted to go on that cruise. I thought it might put a spark or two back in our marriage. She deserved to go on a cruise. She had worked long and hard as a homemaker, a mother and as a professional. She had dreamed about going on a cruise for a long time. But she would not shut up about wanting Steve to go on the trip.

I finally told her that we had the money but if we used it for the mission trip, we would have to postpone the anniversary cruise.

It didn't take her nearly as long to make up her mind as it took me to decide to tell her. She simply said, "I want him to go. We can go on a cruise later. This is probably the only time Steve will have a chance to go on a mission trip with Dr. Hatley." We signed him up.

The next hurdle was getting him a passport. I thought I would just take him down to the post office and get one. I didn't know that we had to have an official birth certificate, fill out papers, get photographs and send the whole package off to New Orleans. The day before he was supposed to leave, the passport came in the mail.

Steve was 15 years old, absolutely full of life and anxious to get into anything and everything that was going on. When he got to Manaus, he ate everything they put in front of him. Later they told him he had eaten monkey, cow's tongue and rat.

One of the ways Dr. Hatley helped his friend Eduardo was to bring young people to Memphis for special training. One young man came to Memphis to learn to fly the small planes used to supply mission outposts. His name was Cesar. He had finished his training and moved back to Brazil. He was a short, mischievous boy with a big grin.

He met the tour group in Manaus and traveled with them down the river. Cesar had lived on the Amazon all his life so he was totally at home on the boat. One of the things he liked to do was to dive off the top of the pilot house into the Amazon River. About the time Cesar hit the water Steve launched himself off the roof of the pilot house. Anything Cesar would do Steve would do.

Dr. Hatley told them not to swim in the Amazon. It was dangerous. The water was fast, the current was strong and there were all kinds of flotsam in the water. There were lots of fish and other kinds of wildlife in the river. Alligators, snakes and Piranha live in the Amazon. Steve didn't worry too much; he probably didn't worry at all. He thought that if Cesar wasn't afraid why should he be afraid?

He was having a great time until one day he saw some men fishing off the back of the boat. They pulled in a large Piranha and he got a good look at its teeth. He didn't swim in the Amazon anymore.

Jim took them to several cities including Rio de Janeiro. Steve said that he really enjoyed the beach at Ipanema. He said that all the bikinis on the entire beach could have been put in one basket.

Several of the people who went on that trip made significant contributions to the cause of missions. Mark and Cindy Morris became professional missionaries and served in Africa, Pakistan and Indonesia.

Steve never gave any indication that he might want to be a missionary, in fact he never wanted to go to college. He said, "Dad, I'll go to college if you make me." I thought that it probably would be a waste of money to send him under those circumstances. In retrospect, I am not sure that was the right decision. Some professor might have turned him on to college and a good education. Even so, his mother and I never regretted sending him to Brazil. I am sure that it opened his eyes and made him a more understanding person.

THE GUN

I WAS ALREADY IN BED EVEN THOUGH IT WAS EARLY; A LITTLE AFTER 9 PM.

I knew I had to get up early the next morning and drive to Louisiana and I had just started a 900 page biography of Winston Churchill. I thought I could probably read for an hour or so before I fell to sleep. I was reading and thinking at the same time. Not that I intended to; it was simply that there was something close to the surface of my subconscious that would not go away. Conscious effort would not pull it up but the distraction of reading allowed it to the surface. Within 10 minutes I knew what was bothering me.

Earlier in the day, I was concerned about antifreeze. I thought it was the 280Z that I have parked in the side yard waiting for enough money to do some engine repairs. I had checked the radiator of the Z to be sure there was antifreeze in it.

When I got comfortable reading about Sir Winston, I remembered that it was the radiator in dad's old Chrysler that had over heated during the summer. I remembered filling the radiator up with water but I could not remember putting in antifreeze.

I tried to tell myself that it was not going to get cold while I was gone but that did not work. The more I thought about it the more I knew that I could not risk a busted radiator or worse still a cracked engine. After a while I knew that the only thing I could do was go to the store and get a gallon of antifreeze and put it in the Chrysler.

I was only 20 steps from the front door of the Piggly Wiggly store when I saw a young man get out of his car and walk toward me. I thought, "He's going to ask for a handout" I kept walking toward the store but he caught up with me before I got there. When he stepped in front of me he pulled a handgun from under his trenchcoat. It was pointed right at my belly button. He said, "Gimme yo money or I'll kill yo." I took my billfold out of my pocket and gave it to him.

Absolutely no hesitation. No thought of heroics. No panic. There wasn't much money in it; barely enough to buy the antifreeze. I thought he's going to be mad when he finds out how little money he got. I was more upset about losing my granddaughter's pictures and having to cancel all the credit cards than I was about losing the money.

I simply stood there and watched him get into the car. There were one or two others in the car and they had it parked with the motor running and in a getaway position. They drove through the parking lot and down the street. I didn't even try to get the license number. I thought, "Don't give the fool a reason to shoot at you." I did make a mental note about the kind of car and a few characteristics of the man.

A man came out of the store just as they drove away. He saw me and I guess I had that startled look on my face. He said, "Did that guy rob you?" I said that he sure did. He said that he could have gotten the tag number but he simply didn't think about somebody pulling a robbery right in front of the store. I somehow didn't care. The robber had gone away and I was alive. Nothing else seemed to matter.

I went into the store and told the manager that I had been robbed and he called the police. It is interesting how calm a person can be when he is threatened by death. I can remember five times, four before this time, that I thought I might die. When I was a teenager I stepped in front of an axe and it cut my thigh almost to the bone. We were miles back in the woods and I thought I might bleed to death before they could get me out. Twice I have been hit head on by an on by an oncoming vehicle on and one time I was trapped under a swamped canoe. None of those events actually threatened my life but for a few moments I thought I might die. Every time I was calm as I could be until it was over. Afterwards I did my share of shaking.

About twenty minutes later the policeman drove up. I suppose the fact that I wasn't hurt and there was no hope of catching the robber destroyed any urgency for him to get to me. I called Mary Jo because I still had to get some antifreeze. She got there at the same time as the policeman and had to wait until he had filled out his report.

There wasn't much I could tell him. I guess I wasn't very observant. He asked me if I would be able to identify the robber and I said, "No, after I saw the gun I didn't see anything else. I did notice features; he was about 5' 9" tall, weighed about 150 pounds, had braided hair and wore a black trench coat. That was about all I remembered except that the car was an old model Cadillac, black with tan vinyl top."

The policeman said, "How big was the gun?" I said, "Big and black." He took out his 45 automatic and asked if it was that big. It wasn't near that big. After some reflection it was probably a 32 automatic. It was not a revolver.

It may not have actually been a big handgun but when it was only three inches from my belly button it sure looked big. Real big. I figured that it would make a big hole in me if he got nervous and pulled the trigger. I've seen a few "belly" shots when I was an operating room technician in the Navy and I know what a mess they can make even if the bullet misses the abdominal aorta.

Mary Jo was not calm. She was furious. She did not have anything civil to say about any part of it. It was a good thing she was not the victim. She might have insulted the robber enough to get shot just to shut her up!

I still had the antifreeze problem. Mary Jo had enough money to buy the antifreeze. I tried to put it into the radiator but I didn't do too good a job of it. I couldn't get the drain cock undone and only got a little into the top of the radiator. I ran the engine for a while and gave up on it.

Later my son said that when we fixed the car last summer we put antifreeze it. I didn't have an antifreeze problem at all. I sure wished I had remembered that earlier. It would have kept me from having a gun problem!

COWBOYS AND INDIANS

ONE OF THE MOST PLEASANT EXPERIENCES OF OUR 1994 VACATION TO Spain was meeting Horacio, who was the Manager (Chef? Owner?) of the "Moncho" restaurant on the beach in the old tourist city of Torremolinos. The area reminded me of the oldest parts of Florida beach cities. There was a long row of souvenir shops, cheap hotels, swim wear shops and restaurants. There must have been 20 restaurants in a 6 block strip. They all looked very much alike.

The first night we were in Spain we stopped at a restaurant that had a small fishing boat full of seafood on ice placed on the sand outside the in front door. There was also a menu written in Spanish, English, German and French. Horacio came over and asked if we spoke English. (Somehow they could all tell, by the way we looked I guess, that we spoke English.) He said that he spoke a little English and a half dozen other languages. He asked if he could show us his "Special Dishes". He said, "I fix you excellent meal - you come in - if you no like what I fix you - you no pay."

I didn't know whether his food was good or not but he certainly was pleasant so we gave it a try. It turned out to be a very good choice. The ambience was not very "up scale" but the food was excellent and Horacio was charming.

Mary Jo is such a people orientated person that the conversation with Horacio was just as important to her as the food. We ate with Horacio three times.

The first night I had Pawns Phil-Phil and Mary Joe had a salad and we both ate Horacio's "Special Dish" which was baked Sea Bass. It was the best piece of fish I had ever eaten.

The second night we went back. Horacio suggested Mussels for our appetizer. I was a little embarrassed that he had to show us how to eat them. He said, "With the fingers - with the fingers." I guess I'm not very much of a finger bowl person. I wasn't sure what that little bowl of water, with the slice of lemon in it, was for. Mary Joe had baked Hake and I had a seafood casserole.

The second week we ate with him again. I had a very fine fish soup, Mary Joe had the Pawns Phil-Phil and for the main course I had Baked Sole and Mary Joe had Sea Bass baked in Salt. She said that her fish was excellent.

The last night I took my journal with me. Horacio was interested in what I had written and was very impressed with the sketches. He asked if he could take them to the back of the restaurant to show to his wife. He said he was planning to come to the U.S. in a year or two and spend a month. We asked him to come to Memphis to see us. I told him that he needed to experience Memphis Barbecue, Fried Catfish, Hushpuppies and Louisiana Gumbo.

LION AT THE "PARTAL" OF THE LADIES
THE ALHAMBRA

10·20·34 AS

I asked him if his wife and bambinos would be coming with him. He said that he didn't have any bambinos and his wife would not come to the U.S. because she was afraid of the violence.

I thought to myself, "There's not that much violence in the United States." Then I remembered that the pain of the World Wars and the Spanish Civil War is still very much with them. I think we forget that their pain is not the memory of rationing, young men gone overseas and newsreels. Their pain was/is absolutely first hand. There is a very definite sensitive place in the European psychic that recoils to violence.

The European view of violence in the United States is exacerbated by the TV we export to them. It seemed to me that there are five kinds of programs on Spanish TV, News, Cultural/environmental programs similar to Discovery or PBS, Game Shows, Sports, and dubbed U.S. Cops and Robber shows. The mildest was Andy Griffin in "Matlock" and even it has to do with crime and murder.

Of course, the O. J. Simpson trial was a significant part of the news - not to the detail it is in the U.S. but still a lot of coverage.

Perhaps we are still a frontier people - enamored with guns and quick to resort to violence. When the more refined part of me wants to say that it is not true I stop short and remember that a man was shot to death inside my office building and that later a young man put a pistol into my belly and demanded my money or my life. It all happened in East Memphis which is definitely not part of the "Black ghetto".

When I stop to think about it we have been brought up on violent entertainment. Even when I was a little boy the radio programs were "The Lone Ranger", "Red Ryder" and "The Shadow." When TV came along, the shows were "Harmless" compared to today's "Blood, gore and sex" but even Fess Parker as "Davey Crockett" and Ed Ames as the Indian in "Daniel Boone" involved guns and killing people. Then there was Bradford Crawford in "The Highway Patrol" and all those guns and robbers shows of the 50's. I suppose Hollywood was and still is playing up to the cowboys and Indian games of our childhood.

The movies from Hollywood are of course more violent than TV. A lot of us are repulsed by the gross violence in movies that are designed to shock the sensibilities of normal people. When you stop and think about it even the "Mainstream Movies" the ones that we think of as "Classics" are full of guns and fighting. John Wayne was our "action" hero of all time. We watch movies like "The sons of Katie Elder" over and over. The machine gunning of Bonnie in "Bonnie and Clyde" is a fixed picture in our minds and we can all see "Butch Cassidy and the Sundance Kid" jumping off the cliff. We flock to see "Rambo" and Chuck Norris movies to the extent that when a non violent movie like "Driving Miss Daisy" comes along it gets an Oscar. The problem is compounded exponentially when we consider the second and third grade movies and movies made for TV.

The problem is that Hollywood gives us what we want. If violent movies did not draw hoards of people, Hollywood would not produce them.

We may be (at least the great majority of us) city people but we still retain our frontier roots. We as a people may give lip service to the Prince of Peace but our souls still belong to the God of War. I wonder how many more generations it will take for the primitive man to give up his desire for killing - ever?

Is there any hope in all of this? Perhaps - perhaps we have made (most of us have made) the small shift from doing violence to viewing violence. We still have a long way to go. It is a long way from vicarious violence to active compassion. Jesus looked upon the crowd with compassion and healed their sick and wounded.

There is the basic flaw in all of us that the Scripture calls "Sin" - but the Scripture also tells us that Christ died that we might live - and live abundantly - with hope - with joy. So, we must believe that the power of God is greater than the power of evil. We must hope that some day people from other countries will not be afraid to visit their friends in America.

INTO THE DEEP

IN 1401, LORENZO GHIBERTI WAS COMMISSIONED TO CREATE THE bronze doors on the east entrance to the Baptistery in Florence. Ghiberti was 25 years old when he started and 74 when he finished. He worked on the doors for 49 years. Michelangelo called them the Gates of Paradise.

What is really important to you? How do you use your ultimate gift, your life? What are you doing with it?

Remember, Jesus provides for all of our needs. He provided wine at the wedding in Cana, bread and fish at the gathering of the 5,000.

Above all, he provides an abundance of grace for whatever the need may be.

Every encounter with Jesus results in the destruction of the unholy and the empowerment of the holy. When Jesus calls there is no telling what might be left behind.

Peter, James and John left their nets full of fish and followed Jesus. At the moment of the biggest catch of fish in their lives, they left it all and followed Jesus.

The greatest fear of our lives should not be that we fail at something important but that we succeed at something insignificant.

Jesus said, "Push out into the deep."

FOUR REASONS

SOMETIMES THE EVENTS OF LIFE MAKE US WONDER WHERE GOD IS hiding.

Sometimes we wonder what happened to the God of Love.

When doubts and fears overwhelm us, we must remind ourselves that there are four reasons our faith must remain strong.

The first reason is the record of God's love in Scripture. There are many gruesome and evil stories in the Bible but they are more than balanced by stories about the glory of God, his miraculous intervention with power and grace and examples of his love. Regardless of man's inhumanity to man the ultimate event is the love of God demonstrated by the sacrificial death of Jesus on the cross.

Second is the history of God's involvement with his church. Through the ages there is a checkerboard of good and evil. The Apostle Paul and the multitude of missionaries that followed him took the Good News to the ends of the earth. Even so, inquisitions and persecutions perpetrated in the name of God, caused pain and death to unnumbered people. Even Galileo was tried for heresy. Still, the Church of God marches forward and the love of God, in spite of all the encumbrances we place upon it, is known by millions of people.

We have also witnessed the power of God in the lives of Contemporary Christians. We have seen lives changed and have seen the Gospel spread to previously unreached areas. We have seen the fall of atheistic empires. The Catholics and Protestants in Ireland have made peace and the Orthodox and Roman Catholics in Bosnia are in an uneasy relationship but in many other places the world is full of conflict and chaos. Apartheid is not the rule of law in South Africa and there is a resurgence of Christianity in Russia. We have witnessed God's power in many ways.

The fourth reason is that we have known the power of God in our own lives. We know what the Apostle Paul was talking about when he said, "While we were yet sinners, Christ died for us." We have experienced the liberating love of God, which we call salvation, and we have experienced the sustaining love of God in the events of our lives. We know that when we falter, as the Prophet said, "All we like sheep have gone astray," our God not only waits for us he woos us back into his fellowship. We therefore testify to the active power of God in our own lives.

So, regardless of how black the circumstances may be, we know that God loves us and though there may be many things we do not understand we can say with Job,

"Though he slay me, still I will trust him."

Halleluiah!
Amen.

GREAT GREAT GRANDPAPPY

THE FIRST BUILDING I DESIGNED AFTER I MOVED TO MEMPHIS IN 1968 was a new Post Office for the city. The award of that design commission from the United States Post Office Department is what allowed Mel O'Brien to add a new design architect to his staff. During the design of the building we went to Washington DC several times. When construction started I was the person who administered the construction contract.

After Richard Nixon was elected president in 1972 he appointed "Red" Blount of Alabama as Postmaster General. Mr. Blount changed the way the Post Office Department managed the construction of buildings. Instead of hiring architects and engineers to manage the construction he turned the responsibility over to the Army Corps of Engineers. They cancelled our contract when the construction of the Memphis Post Office was about twenty-five percent complete.

Even though we had been cut out of the construction phase of the Memphis Post Office we were still very interested in the design phase of future post office buildings. The selection of design architects for this region of the country was handled by the Corps of Engineers division located in Savannah, Georgia. I went to Savannah to talk to the Corps about letting us design another post office building.

The gentleman who interviewed me was Mr. Smith. He was an older gentleman with white hair and a well manicured handlebar mustache. He had twinkling blue eyes and a quick smile. We had a very pleasant conversation and when we were finished I told him that I had enjoyed our visit so much that I wished that I could claim him as a cousin.

One advantage of having the name Smith is that anytime you meet another Smith that you like or that you have a spontaneous affinity with you can claim them as a cousin. Almost anybody in the south can be a distant cousin. Even if the person's name is not Smith there was very likely a Smith somewhere on his mother's side of the family.

Mr. Smith said, "Well, Andrew where are you from? We might be kin; who knows?"

I told him that my clan was from northwest Georgia.

He said that he was from middle Mississippi and we probably were cousins. That statement, of course, startled me. How could we be cousins if he was from Mississippi and my clan was from Georgia?

He said that back before the Civil War his great grand pappy's family lived in the piedmont area of North Carolina. The piedmont got too crowded with newcomers and his great grand pappy and two brothers decided to head west and find a place with more space and not so many neighbors. The three brothers started working their way southwest along the eastern side of the Blue Ridge Mountains. When they got to north Georgia one of the brothers met a pretty young girl and fell in love. The three brothers cleared out a homestead and built a cabin for the new couple. After a couple of years the two bachelor brothers got restless and picked up their duds and started moving to the southwest.

Somewhere around Anniston, Alabama one of the brothers met a girl and got married. This time it was two brothers who cleared out the homestead and built the cabin.

When the third brother got restless he got all the way to middle Mississippi before the same thing happened to him. This time he had to clear his own land and build his own cabin.

Mr. Smith said, "Andrew, we simply left your great grand pappy in north Georgia."

That is such a good story that I wished my great grand pappy had migrated down the eastern slopes of the Blue Ridge Mountains. The fact is that my forbearers came down the western slopes of the mountains. My great grandfather was from Sevier County, Tennessee. He moved to northwest Georgia sometime before the Civil War. That probably meant that his clan of Smiths came from up the Holston River and the Shenandoah Valley of Virginia. Of course there were many people in east Tennessee who came across the Smokies from North Carolina. It could be that Mr. Smith and I are cousins and that it was the "eastern side of the Blue Ridge" part of the story that was wrong.

With a name like Smith you can trace it back many ways and if you trace it far enough you can claim kin to just about anybody.

STUPID ████████████████████████████████████

I know she loves me.
She calls me dirty names.

"Stupid"
"Idiot"
"Dummy"

I WONDER WHAT ELSE SHE WOULD HAVE CALLED ME IF SHE HADN'T looked down the steps and saw that I really was sick.

I was so weak I thought I wasn't going to make it from the airport to the house. It seemed like it took forever for the bags to get to the baggage claim. I sat down in the floor and waited until most of the people had got their bags before I even looked for mine. I think I would have passed out if I had stood at the carousel and waited for the bags.

I had felt pretty good during the day. (Day 3 of the Beijing flue) I had taken enough aspirin to keep the fever down and enough decongestants to dry me up. I had my sister Jeanne, drop me off at the MARTA station and I took the train to the Atlanta airport. I checked my bags so I wouldn't have to fool with them and made the long walk to gate 32 on the B concourse.

By the time I got to the gate I knew my strength was just about gone. My legs were trembling and I was short of breath. I would have been better off if I had gotten a bite to eat but the food at Hartsfield Airport costs so much I almost refuse to buy it on principle. It isn't a matter of the money, it's that I don't like to be ripped off.

I was on the same Sunday night flight I have taken from Atlanta many times. It leaves about 8 PM and I get home about 9 PM.

I was a little late and she was worried. She had called Jean and found out that I had caught the 5 o'clock train and it was now almost 10. She was beginning to think something was wrong.

"Why didn't you call me."

"Why didn't Jeanne take you to the airport?"

"You could have been mugged on that train."

"Doesn't she know that you go bonkers when you get sick?"

When she wasn't calling me names or asking questions she was crying. She rushed down the stairs and started trying to pull me up. It must have looked like a Lucille Ball and Desi Arnez routine.

After I got in the house she picked up the phone and said, "I'll call you back." She had been talking to one of her friends for comfort and reassurance. When she heard the car door slam she put the receiver down and ran to help me.

She helped me get undressed and into the bed, fixed a bowl of soup and spooned it into my mouth. When someone has to feed me you can believe that I am sick!

I was scheduled to leave the next day on another trip and she had taken a week of vacation so she could go with me.

"We're not going."

"You call that office and tell somebody else to go."

"You're going to stay right here."

"I'll take care of you."

Only after I promised her that I would go to the doctor the next morning and that I would cancel the trip if he said I should that she began to calm down.

I woke up about 12:30 AM and realized that my breathing had calmed down. I decided that I had still better go to the doctor. I didn't want to pull a "Jim Henson".

The doctor said that I had a touch of the Beijing flue and gave me a prescription for fifty dollars worth of medicine. He said that it would be alright for me to go on the trip if Mary Jo would go with me.

YOU SURE DO LOOK GOOD

A MAN WAS SHOT AND KILLED IN MY OFFICE BUILDING TODAY. IT appeared to be a robbery. Two young men were seen in the building by several people, including one of my partners. They even talked to one of the men from the Army recruiting office which is on the first floor.

A few moments after they talked to the sergeant in the men's room they went into one of the offices on the first floor and asked the lady where the recruiting office was. When she got up to show them they grabbed her and started taking her jewelry. She screamed and her boss came out of his office to see what was the matter and they shot him through the chest. The bullet must have hit his heart or a large vessel because he collapsed immediately.

The husband of the lady in trouble also worked in that office. He came running to see what was going on and they shot him. One shot hit him in the wrist and another hit him in the upper arm. He ran to the back of the office and out the back door looking for help.

The two assailants ran out the door to the office and turned back toward the center of the building. Why they didn't go out the front door of the building, which was only ten feet away, no one knows. When they got to the middle of the building a man stepped off the elevator right in front of them. One of them pointed a gun right at the man's head but before he could pull the trigger the man dropped to the floor. The gun fired and the shot went over his head, glanced off the wall and struck the wall at the end of the corridor.

The robbers then ran up the open stairway that is directly in front of our office. There are windows between our reception area and the stairway and the first thing I knew our receptionist gave a little yelp and said, "Two men ran up the stairway and one had a gun!" I thought she was imaging things but she said that she heard two gunshots.

Before I could sort it all out one of our young architects came running in the back door to our office. He was pale as a ghost. He was obviously very upset. He said, "I just saw a man get shot out in the parking lot and they shot at me!"

He said he was getting into his car to go get a case of cokes, when a man ran out of the building hollering, "Call 911! Call 911! A man has been shot!" Steve closed the door to his car and started to go see what was wrong when the two men ran out of the building. When they saw Steve one of them raised his gun and pointed it right at Steve's head. Steve said that he was looking right down the barrel. Steve broke and ran toward the corner of the building. The man shot at him but missed. We later found that the bullet had hit a car.

When I heard all this I started toward the back door. Some of the people in the office said "Don't go out there, you might get shot!" But I never slowed down. I remember thinking that whoever had done the shooting had probably ran away and besides if there was someone out there who had been shot I was going to help if I could. I remember wondering if I could remember my CPR training. It had been several years since I had taken the course.

It was a strange feeling. I knew that I was taking a risk. The gunmen might be crazy enough to still be out there. They might shoot at me. I could get shot. Somehow the thought that I might get killed didn't occur to me. I calculated the odds and went on. It is amazing how fast the brain can assimilate information, calculate odds and make a decision. It happens so fast that you don't even know that you are doing it.

When I got back in the office I learned that some of the guys had run downstairs at the same time that I ran out the back door. They said that two men had been shot. One man was in one of the offices downstairs and it looked like he was dying. The other man was on the grass in the front yard.

By the time I got out to the front yard the Medics and the police were there. A whole group of people were around the man on the grass. His wife was there and they were getting ready to load him into the ambulance. The man who died was by this time on his way to the hospital. I understand that he died before they got to the hospital.

It was a tragic day. Makes you realize how arbitrary life is. They could have come into our office. They could have tried to rob our receptionist. She could have screamed. I could have been the man who ran to see what was gong on.

I had just contemplated going out to get a sausage and biscuit but didn't when I realized that I didn't have any money. There are a dozen ways it could have been me in front of the gun.

Would I have dropped like the man in the downstairs hallway? Would I have run? Would I have froze, unable to move? And if I had would my brains be all over the place. I honestly don't know. I think that none of us knows what we will do in life and death situations until we do it. On sober reflection I would not have ran out the back door, but I did.

It sure makes me glad that I am confident in my relationship to God. It makes me appreciate the small blessings of life. The concerns about keeping a business going in a recession and how to stretch the cash flow enough to cover the bills suddenly become insignificant.

I went home and told Mary Jo that I had never seen a more beautiful woman in my entire life. I said, "You sure do look good to me!"

NOT YOUR PROBLEM

NOT LONG AFTER HURRICANE KATRINA HIT THE GULF COAST MY SON Steve said, "Dad, why can't our church send people to New Orleans and build a house instead of building a Habitat house in Memphis?" (Our church had sponsored and built several Habitat houses.) I told him there was no reason at all. He wanted to know what he could do to make it happen. I suggested he talk to everyone he knew who had been involved in the building of the Habitat houses and to talk to anybody he knew in the construction industry.

Our church has a house for missionary families on furlough. It was not occupied so it was opened up for families displaced by the storm. I thought we might go to New Orleans and work on the home of the family who was living the church's Mission House. I spoke to the husband in the family. Eventually he found a good job in Memphis and decided to not go back to New Orleans.

Early in February I heard that a group from the church was going to Pearlington, Mississippi to help rebuild homes. I am sure that all the time Steve and I were looking for a way to help, others were doing the same thing. Somebody contacted the Cooperative Baptist Fellowship and found that CBF had set up a camp in Pearlington to coordinate volunteers from CBF churches. CBF sent word that they had an opening in March for 30 workers. Steve was the first person to sign up.

I told them I would help. I wanted to support Steve and I wanted to do what I could do. I wasn't sure how many days I could get off work. I have also reached an age that prevents me from doing as much physical work as I used to do. The third factor was that I have had a chest cold for several weeks. I have not been able to get over it. All of that combined to limit my participation.

Pearlington is on the Mississippi side of the Pearl River, which is the boundary between Mississippi and Louisiana. It is about 6 miles inland and 9 feet above sea level. The tiny town was directly in the path of the eastern wall of the eye of the hurricane.

A week or so before the time to leave I realized I had not recovered from my cold. I was still coughing, especially when I encountered a new environment. I thought, "I'm not sure I can handle sleeping on a cot in a tent or in an abandoned school room with 30 or so other men." I got on the Internet and eventually found a motel room in Hattiesburg, Mississippi, which is about an hour and a half north of Pearlingtom. They wanted about twice as much as the room would normally cost but I reserved it anyway. I knew that it would not be smart to leave Memphis at 1 pm, drive all the way to the coast and then try to find a place to sleep.

Steve left Memphis early Wednesday morning. He normally gets up about 4 am. He put every tool he owned and some he borrowed into the back of his pickup truck. He had nail guns, air compressors, chain saws and boxes of hand tools. He also had a tent, a folding cot and his sleeping bag. One of the most important items was a cooler with a 12 pack of Bud. He said that he knew that he was part of a church group but that didn't mean he could not have an "adult" beverage now and then.

Steve called about 6 pm Wednesday to tell me he had been assigned to help rebuild a house for a man named Ken Short. He had been on the job 4 hours and had framed some rooms, run some electrical wire and installed some plumbing fixtures. He was happy. He would have done anything they asked him to do but he really wanted to build something.

FEMA had delivered a trailer to Ken's lot that day and that was where he was going to sleep. Ken and his wife, Cathi, were living in a mobile home in Slidell, Louisiana. We agreed that when I got to Pearlington I would find him and be his helper.

I left Memphis a little after 1 pm and pulled into Hattiesburg about 6 pm. After some searching I found the motel and a Cracker Barrel. Steve called to tell me that he was making good progress on Ken's house. He was working with Ken and the others from the church were working somewhere else. I am sure he preferred it that way. (It is not that he didn't want to work with others, it is simply that there are few people who work a hard or as quickly as Steve.) Somehow he got an "overdrive gear" that most people do not have. Those who work with or for Steve either, "get with it," or they "get out of the way." His employees either, "do it his way" or they, "hit the highway."

The next morning, when I began to see demolished houses, I called him. He told me where he was working and I tried to find him. I got totally lost. There were no street signs and some of the streets were blocked by large piles of debris. After making 3 or 4 wrong turns I stopped. I called him and told him that I was next to a playground. He said for me to wait right there and he would come get me. I was within 3 blocks of Ken's house but didn't know where I was.

Ken and Cathi have lived in Pearlington for over 20 years. He worked as a SCUBA diver and an underwater welder. He worked on oil rigs in the Gulf and for refineries on the coast. In recent years he has developed sleep apnea, which prevents him from making deep dives so he is now a supervisor. Cathi works for a bank in Slidell. .

They had a 12 foot wide by 40 foot long mobile home set up on concrete blocks about 3 feet off the ground. For as long as anybody could remember that elevation had been adequate to protect from flooding. He said that the most water he had ever seen in Pearlington was about 2 feet deep.

They watched the storm develop for several days and finally realized that Pearlington was going to be very close to the eye of the storm. Ken told Cathi to get what she could into her truck and he would put some stuff in his because they were leaving. They had no idea that their home would be destroyed. They expected high winds but they never expected the storm surge to go right over the top of their home. Had they known the damage would be from water they would have taken more stuff or perhaps different stuff. For example, Ken is a writer and has several published short stories. He would definitely have taken his computers. The published stories were preserved but the unpublished and the work in progress was on his hard drives. It doesn't take a lot of salt water to destroy a computer hard drive.

They got out. They were a hundred miles away when the storm hit. Ken said that water from the storm surge was about 27 feet high when it passed over his house.

By the time Ken was able to chain saw his way to his house it was not only trashed with muddy water, it was covered with mold. He was able to salvage a few things that were not subject to water damage but everything else was worthless. All the soft goods, clothes, bedding, furniture and all paper goods, books, papers and photographs etc. simply had to be carried out to the street.

Sometime later, perhaps in January, a group of churchmen arrived one day and said that they were there to demolish his house. It was a very emotional day. Part of the time he helped them and part of the time he went out into the woods and cried. It didn't take them long. In a short period of time 32 years of Ken and Cathi's life was piled up on the street waiting for a front-end loader and a dump truck to take it to a land fill.

I will make no attempt to tell about Ken's struggle with FEMA, The Corps of Engineers and the Small Business Administration.

As I understand it FEMA offered him $10,500 for his mobile home. He thought that was a fair price. After all, the home was over 20 years old. The problem was that the $10,500 was tied to a $65,000 loan and he could not have the $10,500 without accepting the loan and paying all the interest. He told them that he did not need $65,000; the $10,500 grant was all he needed. No way. He could not have the grant without the loan. He told them to shove it. He would rebuild with his own resources.

Ken is a man of many talents. He knows how to build almost anything. In December he drew up plans for his house including wiring and plumbing schematics a material list and production schedule. The plan was simple. He intended to use as much salvaged material as possible but he wanted to build a stronger building that could be easily repaired in the event of another floor.

After they moved the remains of his home to the street, there was nothing left but the trailer frame and some concrete blocks. He talked the Building Official into giving him a "Reconstruction Permit" and began salvaging lumber, building materials and anything else he could use from demolished houses. With his meager savings he went to Baton Rouge, Hattiesburg or anywhere that had lumber and bought 2 x10's and plywood.

By January 28th He and Cathi had installed the first floor joists. A group of volunteers from John's Creek Baptist Church in Aalpharetta, Georgia showed up to help. All of the floor joists, the plywood floor and two stud walls were up by the end of the day.

The group from John's Creek signed the end floor joist. I told him that I was the grandfather of John's Creek Baptist. I went on to explain that many years ago I was the lay pastor of a small church north of Atlanta called Dunwoody Baptist Church. That church eventually became a large church that established several missions. One of those missions became John's Creek Baptist Church. That, in a sense, makes me the grandfather.

He could not count the number of church groups that came to work on his house. He never knew who was coming or what they could do but they all worked. Sometimes it would be a group of men who had experience in construction and sometimes it was a bunch of teenagers who did not know one end of a hammer from the other..

The next group built 2 x 4 stud walls and stood them up along the edges of the platform. Then came rafters, roof sheathing and a metal roof. By the time I got there the exterior siding, windows, doors, insulation and some interior paneling had been installed. I'm not sure how much was new material and how much was salvaged but it was obvious that he was making the best of a bad situation.

Cathi's job at the bank disappeared when her employer decided to move from New Orleans to Texas but she was able to find employment with another local bank. For the first time in his life Ken began to draw unemployment. They had a few dollars saved and they arranged for a small signature loan from Cathi's bank.

It didn't take long for me to realize that Ken is a world-class talker. He is one of those men with whom you can have a daylong conversation and not say more than a dozen words. We walked around the property and he told me the whole story about rebuilding his home. I looked at all the stuff he had salvaged. Lumber of all sizes, concrete block, foundation pads, steps, windows, mirrors and doors. He said that anything he could not use somebody else could.

I quickly got a signal from Steve that said that the more I talked with Ken, or to be more accurate, the more I listened to Ken, the more work he could do.

After and hour or so Ken said, "Get your camera and let me take you around and show you some things." We started out driving around his immediate neighborhood. He knew everybody and we stopped to talk to all of them. One neighbor's wife had died since the storm and another had had been in a bicycle accident. She was all skinned up and not in good shape. Another man was still fighting with FEMA. He chatted with all of them. He promised to bring the bicycle lady a washing machine. Where he was going to get it I do not know.

It appears that the storm surge, which was higher on the eastern wall of the eye of the hurricane than anywhere else, came right up the Pearl River. The marshland between Pearlington and the coast slowed the water down but the river offered no resistance. By the time the surge got to Pearlington the water was 32 feet high. That wall of water came rushing through the city and wiped away everything that was not anchored securely to the ground.

Pearlington was home to retirees, people who worked in New Orleans and a few who worked in the refineries or at the John Stenis Complex. Many of the retirees lived in mobile homes, double wides or in Jim Walter type prefabricated homes. Almost all of those structures were destroyed. Many were picked up and moved off their foundations.

There was also a community of about 65 relatively expensive homes south of US 90 and east of the Pearl River. There was not a single one of those homes left. They were not simply damaged they were gone! Nothing was left but slabs or pilings. There was a whole row of pilings standing like snags left after a forest fire. The debris was scattered over a mile of woods and swamps. Ken said that he has been examining houses since the storm and that the hydraulic effect of the incoming waves tore one inch diameter bolts out of the pilings

It was interesting that, in the older part of the city, some of the houses that survived the storm were built over 100 years ago. They were securely connected to good foundations, constructed with excellent lumber, sheathed with 1 X 6's and either paneled or plastered on the inside. Back then there was no plywood or gypsum board. They did not have batt insulation so the mould and mildew problem was not as serious. When the water drained away the wood dried and much of it went back to its original condition. The older houses were damaged and the interiors will have to be rebuilt but the exteriors survived.

A large tugboat was sitting on dry land a mile or so upstream from the highway bridge. The bridge is not a high above the river. The boat could not have gone under it. It had to have floated over the bridge. They don't know who owns it or where it came from.

There was significant damage to the trees and foliage but it was not like the path of a tornado or the flank of Mt. St. Helen.

We stopped at the Presbyterian camp and talked to a the lady who was the cook. (She had offered to cook for the Baptist but they wouldn't have her because she is a Muslim.) Why she was there or who sent her I do not know. I understand she showed up several weeks ago looking for some way to help.

She said, "Oh Ken, do you need any more lumber?" We went over to look at a large pile of lumber that had been cleaned, i.e. the nails had been removed etc. "Come and get any of this you need and tell your neighbors about it." Then she said, "What about your refrigerator?" Ken told her that it was gone. He didn't know whether it floated away or whether it was part of the trash. She said, "We'll deliver one to you this afternoon." He wanted to know how much he owed and how to write the check. She assured him that he didn't owe anybody anything.

He said that a new water heater showed up the same way. He was talking to one of the church groups and one of the men told him the brown box sitting in his trailer was a new water heater. Ken told them he had not ordered a water heater. They said they knew he needed one so they sent one out to him.

All of the disappointment and frustration with government assistance is, in some measure, offset by the response from church groups and simply from people who want to help.

After we had talked to all the neighbors, toured the city to see the destruction and visited with the church groups Ken said, "You are a man of the cloth; I want to show you Logtown." On the way out to Logtown he told me that in the 1850's Logtown was the largest sawmill in the world. Much of the virgin timber in southern Mississippi was floated down the Pearl River and processed into lumber at Logtown. We drove out north of the city and took a road to the west toward the Pearl River. There was nothing along the road except centuries old live oaks and an old cemetery. We came to a clearing on the riverbank and he stopped and said, "Let's get out." We walked over to the edge of the river and he said, "This is where I came back to the Lord."

That is when I realized why I was in Pearlington. I had not been sent down there to do carpentry work. I had been sent to "Listen" to a man who was struggling to find his way back to his Lord.

He began to tell the story of being a Marine in Vietnam. He was sent on a RECON mission. All of his men except for one had been killed and both he and his buddy were wounded. He disappeared into the night with his kaybar knife, infiltrating the enemy and began the grisly task of "kill or be killed." He said they were all good men. They just happened to be on the opposite sides of a political coin. The killing part was easy, that was exactly what he was trained to do. Living with what he had to do was the hard part.

The stress of Katrina and a long-standing friction between him and his in-laws pushed him to the brink of forgetting his vow. He got his Government Issue 9 mm pistol and started up the road with the intent of killing his in-laws. Somehow he found himself down on the bank of the river at Logtown. He struggled with himself for quite some time, perhaps like Jacob struggling with the angel. Eventually he came to the point where he said, "Lord I'm not going to do it." He said he had not talked to the Lord for in 30 years.

He went back into town, found Mary Jo Dean, a minister with the Red Cross and told her that he needed to surrender his weapon to a police officer.

He has been back to church a few times since then. He said that he had not gone to church very much because they were all a bunch of hypocrites. I thought for a moment and said, "Ken that is not your problem. Remember, the church is full of imperfect people and when you go to church it is even more imperfect. There are hypocrites in the church. There have always been hypocrites in the church. You are not responsible for their hypocrisy." He said, "I've never thought about it like that."

By the time we got back to the trailer it was time for lunch. Cathi had been to Slidell and brought back Subway sandwiches.

I gave him a little construction advice about strapping his floor joists to his I beam frame and told him that he should cross brace the posts under his porch. A little later, the leader of the men from the church called and said that they were closing up and heading home. I helped Steve pick up his tools and we started north.

It was an interesting trip. Steve worked 4 days and made a lot of progress on the construction of Ken and Cathi's home. I was there ½ day and listened to the saga of Ken's return to the Lord. I am going to send him Dr. Hatley's book, "You Can Go Home Again." I hope I was able to help him as much in his spiritual journey as Steve helped him with the reconstruction his home.

VERNON GREEN

Vernon and Norma Green had been our next door neighbors for many years. They had just returned from Leesburg, Florida where they had spent the Christmas holidays with their daughter.

He came back with a cold. Norma had talked to Mary Jo several times. She said she was worried about him but he would not go to the doctor. She finally talked to the doctor and he sent out some medicine. She took care of him for several days but he did not get any better.

When the telephone rang about 4 am I knew there was a problem. Norma said his breathing had become so difficult she called 911. They took him to St. Francis Hospital.

I began to be more concerned when she called later to tell us that he was in ICU with double pneumonia. She was upset because they would not let her stay with him. I asked her if I could sit with her or if I could go with her to see Vernon. She said that they had him "all doped up" and he probably wouldn't recognize either one of us.

The next day she got a room in the hospital, on the floor right above the ICU. She said that he was doing some better and that she hoped he would be in a regular room soon.

The following day, about 6 pm, the phone rang. Mary Jo said, "It's Norma and she wants to talk to you." She said, "We've lost Vernon." After the normal questions: When? What happened? I thought he was much better? She said, "His heart just stopped. Can you come?"

I rushed to St. Francis and found her in a little room reserved for grieving families. I gave her a big hug. She is a small woman. It was like comforting a child.

I said all the normal things. I never say that it was God's will or that God loved him more that we did. I told her that God gave us imperfect bodies and that in time they fail and that in most cases it is before we are ready. That was true even in Vernon's case and he was 83 years old. I try to reassure people that God loves them regardless of life's circumstances.

We had about 15 minutes together. She told me about her decision to stop CPR. They told her that he would be brain damaged even if he survived. I affirmed her decision and let her sob a little.

Soon her friends began to arrive. First was a couple and then a "Take charge type lady." "Now Norma, you've got to do this and Norma, you've got to do that, etc." I learned that the lady's husband died last year and that Norma had been a great comfort to her. Now the lady was repaying the debt.

I was about to make my exit when a nurse came in. She said, "Ms. Green, we have cleaned him up and removed all the tubes and equipment. You can go see him before the funeral home takes him away."

Norma said, "I don't think I want to do that. I'd rather remember him alive." Her friend said, "Norma, you've got to do this. It is important that you know that he is dead." "I'll go with you." I thought, "Now, this is the perfect time for me to ease out." Norma took my arm and said, "You come with me." I had no choice but to go with her.

I stood beside the new widow and put my arm around her. She gave another little sob and turned to me and said, "You pray."

I had not anticipated being asked to pray. When you know that you are, or that you might be asked to pray, you can make some preparation. You can have a little something in your mind. Her request took me totally by surprise.

It is amazing how many thoughts can go through your brain in those few seconds between the request and the time you have to say something. What do I know about Vernon and Norma that would be helpful to this little woman? What do I say in these circumstances that would have any significance?

I don't remember exactly what I said but I gave thanks for the life of Vernon Green, for his parents and for all those who loved him. I gave thanks for those who taught and cared for him when he was growing up and for those who sustained him throughout his life. I gave thanks for the love and sacrifice of Jesus Christ who died for Vernon's salvation. I gave thanks for Vernon's opportunity to use his life in service to his church. I gave thanks for the special love he and Norma had for each other and for their long life together. I closed by asking for the comfort of the Holy Spirit during the difficult days ahead.

I stood, one arm around the widow and one hand on the dead man's arm, composing a prayer and breathing another prayer every time I paused. "Lord help me say something helpful."

When I said "Amen" Norma said, "That was exactly what I needed." "Let's go." She walked out confident and assured. She never looked back.

The next day Norma said, "Could you go to Kansas with us and do the ceremony at the graveside?" I stammered a bit and said that I probably could make arrangements if it was necessary.

She said that she could not find a "Latter Day Saints" preacher. Vernon was from Independence, Missouri and had been brought up in the Latter Day Saints Church. He and Norma had attended the Presbyterian Church in Memphis but it was understood that he would be buried in Independence.

I made a few suggestions about how she might find someone and then said, "You don't have to have a preacher for a graveside service." She said, "You don't?"

I told her about the time I forgot the funeral. When I finally found the family and apologized, I asked the nephew of the lady who had died what they did when I did not show up. He said, "I was a major in the army in Korea and I had to bury a lot of soldiers. I still had my army New Testament in my pocket. I took it out and read from John 14 and said a prayer." "We said good-by and buried our Aunt Margret." I said, "That is all I would have done."

Norma said, "That is exactly what we will do." "We don't need no Latter Day Saints preacher."

When she got back from Independence I asked her how it went, she said, "Fine, just fine. One of Vernon's nieces is a reader in the Catholic Church so I asked her to read the Scripture. One of his nephews is a Deacon, so I asked him to say the prayer." That was all that needed to be done and we did it.

POSTSCRIPT

THERE ARE TIMES WHEN YOU GET A WAKE UP CALL. ON DECEMBER 5, 2018, we were in the hospital where Mary Jo was recovering from a fall which cracked two bones in her neck. She also got a call from her brother. who told her that her sister-in-law, Jo Anne had died. You start thinking about the aging process.

The only alternative to dealing with the infirmities of old age is to die young and none of us want that option. (There are, of course, a few who choose to terminate life early but that is an illness we consider a tragedy.) As we get older we not only have to deal with our own diminishing strength and vitality we have to watch the lives of our friends fade away.

How do we honor the lives of our family and the friends we have known and loved for many years? When you reach your eighties many friends have died with cancer, heart attacks, or other illnesses. Others have slipped away into never never land - many of years of memory gone or dimming ever so slowly. Years of love, sacrifice and hard work – gone. Years of devotion, commitment and ministry – gone. Years of caring and providing for children, grand children and great grand children - gone. Years of teaching children in Sunday School, Choir, Vacation Bible School, Church Camp and other ministries – gone. A lifetime relegated to the pages of history.

During the last decade, thirty two, (that I can remember) friends, in our age group, have died. Four have lost all or almost all contact with their former lives. Five others are dealing with Altzimers's or Parkinson's disease.

So far we are survivors and we have been blessed. There have been hardships and disappointments, but there have been joyful times as well. We have reached the point in life where we do not pray for strength to run the marathon; we are content to pray for peace and understanding. We are dealing with falls, loss of hearing, fading eyesight, failing kidneys, cancer, dementia, loss of memory and other infirmities of old age.

What do we do? How do we honor our friends and maintain meaning in life? We pray for strength to meet the future with dignity, and the courage to use whatever strength and time we have left to love, to support our family, our friends and those who need us.

We must be alert; keep our eyes open and listen for the small voice of the Comforter. We must remember that the Comforter is also the Challenger. We may be old and battered but that does not mean we cannot serve our Lord when the opportunity to serve is presented to us.

Remember that the call to be a servant in the Kingdom can come at any minute.

Be ready when your name is called.

No matter the circumstances, we are blessed.

Praise the Lord.

When I wrote these reflections I did not know how soon it would be before I would add Mary Jo's name to the list of those who had died. One week before she died, I was out looking for another Rehab facility where she could fully recover. I knew she had a serious heart condition and I knew she had just recovered from pneumonia but I expected her to live. I had many plans for the rest of our lives.

We will not get to take another trip to Europe. (I wanted so much to take her to Florence and show her the architecture and art of Leonardo De Vinci and Michelangelo.) We would not get to celebrate the birthdays of our great grandchildren. We would not get to watch the sun set again over the red rocks of Sedona.

I not only lost her love and companionship, I lost the plans and dreams for our future.

The abrupt change in dreams is what is so devastating.

Andrew L. Smith

Printed in the United States
By Bookmasters